550 RS908 m

27.04.99

◁ **Overleaf** A sunset over rocks near Flagstaff, Arizona, U.S.A. Sedimentary rocks like these are formed from the remains of other rocks.

◀ **This blue iceberg,** from Alaska, has been carved into amazing shapes by the wind and waves. It will also change shape as it melts, although this can take years. It can travel up to 26 kilometres a day.

YOUR WORLD EXPLAINED

Earth

An accessible guide that *really*
explains our planet

BARBARA TAYLOR

MARSHALL PUBLISHING • LONDON

A Marshall Edition
Conceived, edited and designed by
Marshall Editions Ltd
The Orangery
161 New Bond Street
London W1Y 9PA

First published in the UK in 1997 by Marshall Publishing Ltd
This edition published in 1998

ISBN: 1-84028-156-1

Editor: Louisa Somerville
Designer: John Jamieson
Design Manager: Ralph Pitchford
Managing Editor: Kate Phelps
Art Director: Branka Surla
Editorial Director: Cynthia O'Brien
Production: Janice Storr, Selby Sinton
Research: Lynda Wargen
Picture Research: Zilda Tandy

Originated in Singapore by Master Image
Printed and bound in Portugal by Printer Portuguesa

Contents

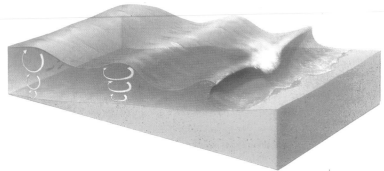

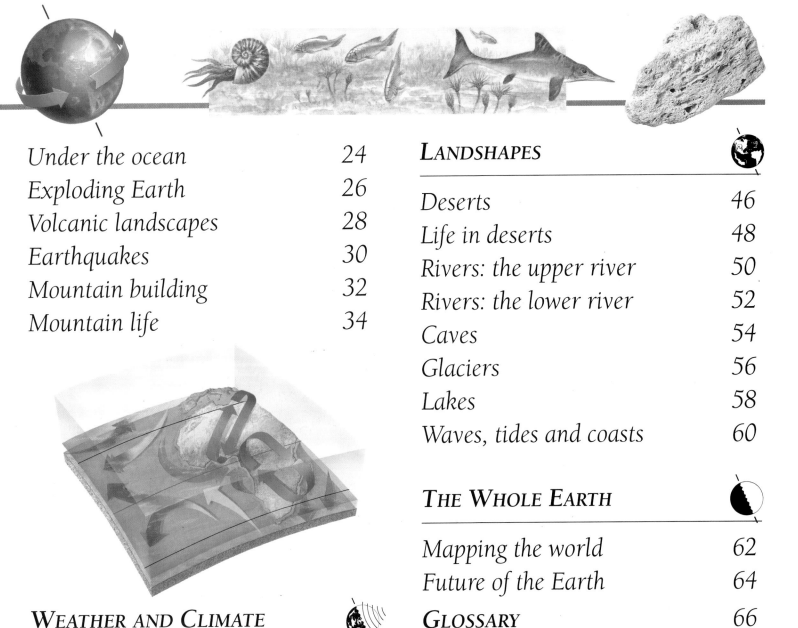

LANDSHAPES

THE WHOLE EARTH

GLOSSARY

INDEX

WEATHER AND CLIMATE

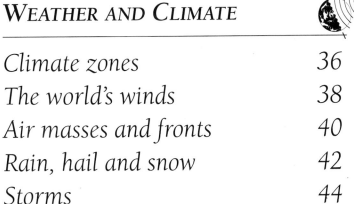

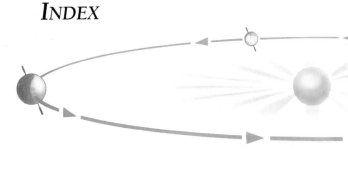

THE FORCES THAT SHAPE THE EARTH

FROM VOLCANOES AND EARTHQUAKES TO RIVERS AND THE weather, everything that happens to the Earth is linked to two major forces: heat and the pulling of gravity. The heat comes from the Sun and also from inside the Earth.

The changing Earth

The Earth we live on is changing all the time. Mountains are being pushed up, continents are sliding around on the surface, and wind and water are carving the land into new shapes.

All these changes are brought about by two heat "engines", one working inside the Earth and one working outside. They are called "engines" because – like the engine of a car – they convert heat energy into movement energy.

▲ **The Sun** is a ball of incredibly hot gas, with temperatures in the middle reaching 15 million°C. The Sun is far enough away from the Earth for its heat to warm the planet without burning it.

▼ **Heat from the Sun** warms the Earth and drives its external heat engine. Without the Sun's heat, the Earth would be an icy, lifeless desert. Heat from inside the Earth pushes and pulls the crust up and down, making the rocks on the surface move.

heat from the Sun

volcano

crust

▲ **This view of Earth** from the Moon reminds us that the Earth is only a tiny blue globe in the blackness of space.

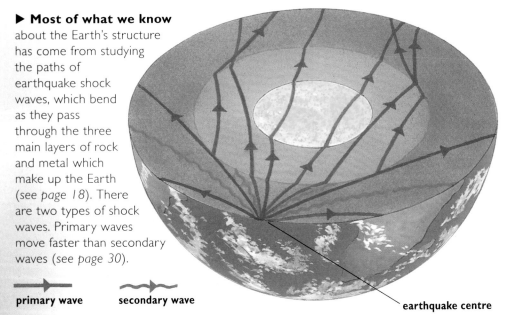

▶ **Most of what we know** about the Earth's structure has come from studying the paths of earthquake shock waves, which bend as they pass through the three main layers of rock and metal which make up the Earth (see *page 18*). There are two types of shock waves. Primary waves move faster than secondary waves (see *page 30*).

➤ primary wave   〜 secondary wave

earthquake centre

Twin engines
The "engine" inside the Earth is powered by heat rising from the hot centre, called the core, toward the Earth's surface, or crust. Heat from the engine pushes the crust up, moves it around and tears it apart. Mountains, volcanoes and the drifting of the continents are all caused by this moving heat.

The heat engine outside the Earth is powered by the Sun. The Sun's heat causes movement in a blanket of gases surrounding the Earth, called the atmosphere. This movement makes winds blow. The Sun's heat also makes water from the Earth's surface rise into the atmosphere and fall to Earth as rain, in a process known as the water cycle (*see pages 11 and 42*). This constant movement of wind and water over the Earth's surface wears away the land in some places and builds it up in others.

The pulling force
The Earth's gravity stops things from flying off into space by pulling them toward the Earth's centre. Gravity makes rivers flow downhill and makes rain fall to the ground.

Earth is round because of gravity. Every part of the Earth is pulling every other part toward the centre, creating a sphere – the best shape for packing things together.

The pull of Earth's gravity holds the Moon in place, and the Sun's gravity keeps the Earth and all the other planets circling around it.

▲ **When astronauts float free** high above the Earth, they feel weightless; yet the Earth's gravity is still stopping them from flying off into deep space.

clouds and weather

moving ocean floor

Earth's surface

mountains forming

moving continents

heat inside the Earth

Shaping the surface

The changes that are going on inside the Earth are hard to imagine because we cannot see them. Changes on the Earth's surface are more obvious because we experience them daily. These changes include the weather, and the way rivers, glaciers and oceans alter the shape of the land. All surface changes are driven by the Sun's heat and by the force of gravity (*see pages 8–9*).

The Sun warms the middle of the Earth, around the equator, more than the poles. This makes hot air rise near the equator and sink near the poles, creating a pattern of global winds (*see pages 38–39*). In turn, these winds drive ocean currents. Global winds and ocean currents spread heat around the Earth and bring about changes in the world's weather.

WEATHERING AND EROSION

Rock on the Earth's surface is broken down by a process called weathering. Mechanical weathering happens when rocks that heat up by day and cool down at night start to crack and crumble. Chemical weathering happens when rocks are eaten away by chemicals, such as the acids in rain.

Pieces of weathered rock loosen and are carried away by the wind, the ice in glaciers, or the water in rivers or oceans. This process is known as erosion. As the rock debris is carried along, it grinds against the Earth's surface, wears it away and changes the shape of the land.

wind erosion in a desert

water erosion by a river

ice erosion by a glacier

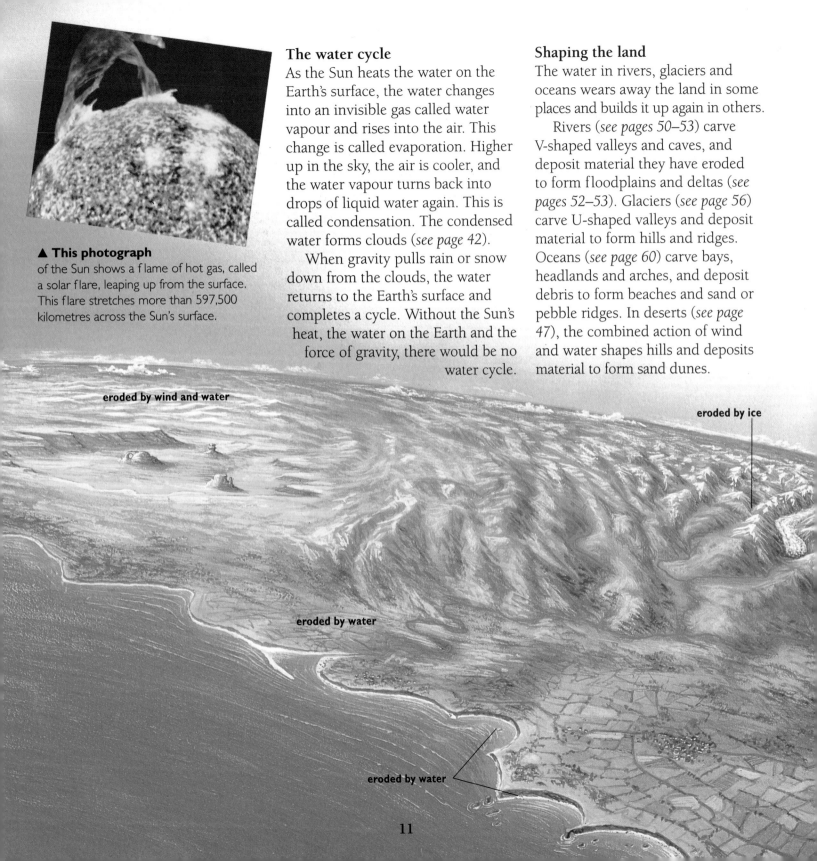

▲ This photograph
of the Sun shows a flame of hot gas, called a solar flare, leaping up from the surface. This flare stretches more than 597,500 kilometres across the Sun's surface.

The water cycle

As the Sun heats the water on the Earth's surface, the water changes into an invisible gas called water vapour and rises into the air. This change is called evaporation. Higher up in the sky, the air is cooler, and the water vapour turns back into drops of liquid water again. This is called condensation. The condensed water forms clouds (*see page 42*).

When gravity pulls rain or snow down from the clouds, the water returns to the Earth's surface and completes a cycle. Without the Sun's heat, the water on the Earth and the force of gravity, there would be no water cycle.

Shaping the land

The water in rivers, glaciers and oceans wears away the land in some places and builds it up again in others.

Rivers (*see pages 50–53*) carve V-shaped valleys and caves, and deposit material they have eroded to form floodplains and deltas (*see pages 52–53*). Glaciers (*see page 56*) carve U-shaped valleys and deposit material to form hills and ridges. Oceans (*see page 60*) carve bays, headlands and arches, and deposit debris to form beaches and sand or pebble ridges. In deserts (*see page 47*), the combined action of wind and water shapes hills and deposits material to form sand dunes.

eroded by wind and water

eroded by ice

eroded by water

eroded by water

THE SUN'S FAMILY

THE EARTH IS ONE OF A GROUP OF NINE PLANETS made up of rock, metal and gases. Each planet journeys, or orbits, around the Sun. Earth is the only one of the planets that is known to support life.

close-up of dust and gas particles

The Earth in space

No one knows for sure how the Earth was formed. But many astronomers believe that it started about 4.6 billion years ago from spinning clouds of dust and gas left over after the birth of the Sun.

Dust and gases may have stuck together to form four solid planets: Mercury, Venus, Earth and Mars. Farther away from the Sun, dust and gases may have clumped together to make the gas planets: Jupiter, Saturn, Uranus, Neptune and Pluto. It took several million years for the Sun and the planets to form.

The huge Universe
Earth, the Sun and the other planets are only a minute part of the whole vast Universe, which is everything that exists – including rock, air, water, people, animals, plants, stars, planets and moons. The Universe is so massive that light from stars far away takes billions of years to reach Earth.

00:00:00	Big Bang
17:00:00	Solar system formed
23:59:30	First humans
23:59:59	Now

▲ **Imagine the history of the Universe** happened in 24 hours. If the Big Bang was 24 hours ago, the Sun and planets were born 7 hours ago, and the first humans appeared only in the last 30 seconds.

▶ **On the young Earth,** the seas were still hot, electrical storms raged in the clouds, and volcanoes threw ash and lava on to the surface. Eventually the surface cooled. Simple forms of life appeared in the oceans about 3 billion years ago (see page 14).

▲ **Blowing up a balloon** like this shows that if the Universe (the balloon) is expanding, then the galaxies (the stuck-on stars) must be moving away from one another.

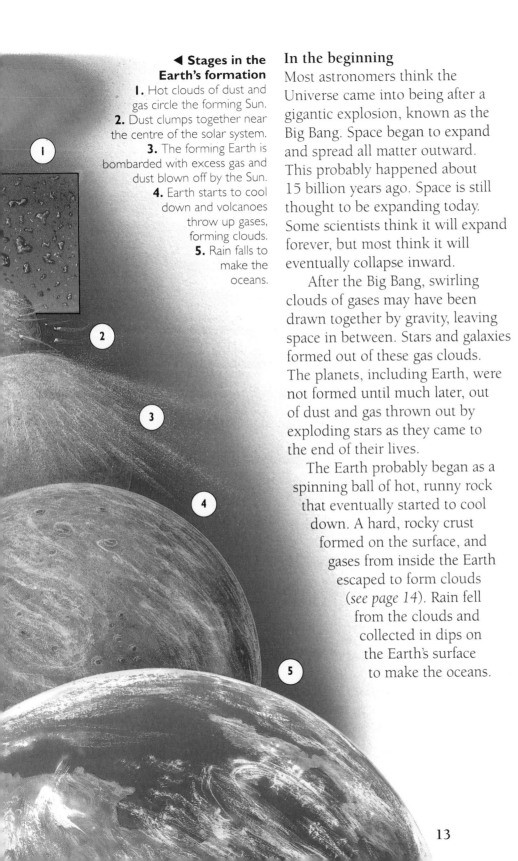

◄ Stages in the Earth's formation
1. Hot clouds of dust and gas circle the forming Sun.
2. Dust clumps together near the centre of the solar system.
3. The forming Earth is bombarded with excess gas and dust blown off by the Sun.
4. Earth starts to cool down and volcanoes throw up gases, forming clouds.
5. Rain falls to make the oceans.

In the beginning

Most astronomers think the Universe came into being after a gigantic explosion, known as the Big Bang. Space began to expand and spread all matter outward. This probably happened about 15 billion years ago. Space is still thought to be expanding today. Some scientists think it will expand forever, but most think it will eventually collapse inward.

After the Big Bang, swirling clouds of gases may have been drawn together by gravity, leaving space in between. Stars and galaxies formed out of these gas clouds. The planets, including Earth, were not formed until much later, out of dust and gas thrown out by exploding stars as they came to the end of their lives.

The Earth probably began as a spinning ball of hot, runny rock that eventually started to cool down. A hard, rocky crust formed on the surface, and gases from inside the Earth escaped to form clouds (*see page 14*). Rain fell from the clouds and collected in dips on the Earth's surface to make the oceans.

(*see page 14*)

THE EARTH IN THE UNIVERSE

To us the Earth is vitally important, but in terms of the whole Universe, it is only a tiny speck among billions of stars, planets, moons and other bits of space debris.

The Earth is one of nine planets in our solar system, with the Sun, a star, at the centre. The Sun is just one of about 100 billion stars in a galaxy called the Milky Way. (The Milky Way looks like a glowing band of light in the night sky.) It is part of a group of about 30 galaxies. There are thousands of millions of galaxies in the Universe.

Earth is the fifth-largest planet in the solar system. It has one moon.

The Sun, planets, moons, comets, asteroids and space debris together make up the solar system.

A galaxy is a huge cluster of billions of stars and planets.

The Universe probably consists of about 100 billion galaxies.

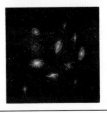

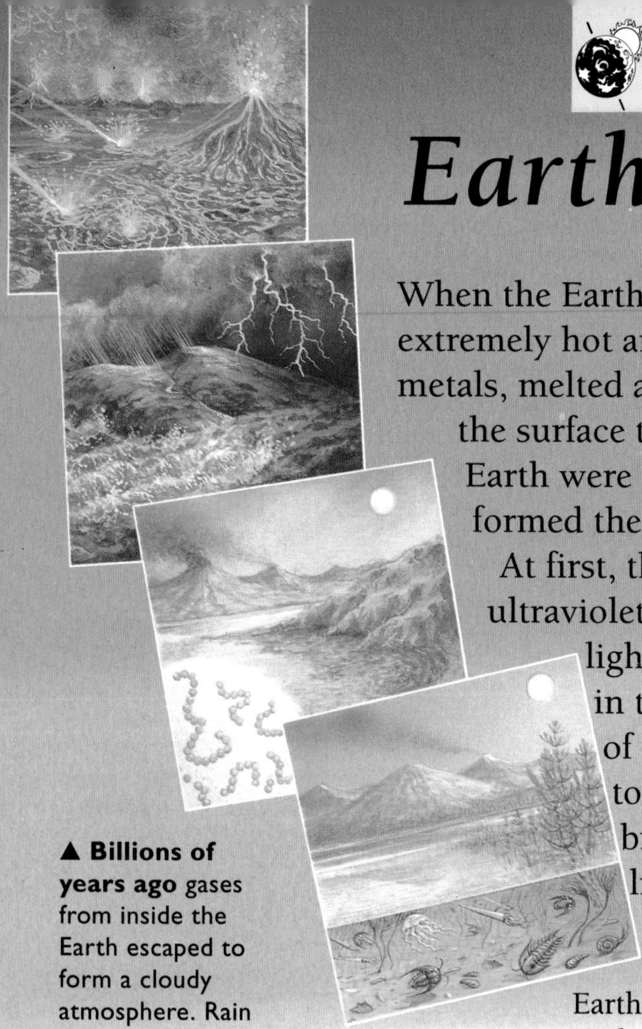

Earth's atmosphere

When the Earth first formed about 4.6 billion years ago, it was extremely hot and there was no life. Iron and nickel, which are heavy metals, melted and sank to form the core. Lighter rocks floated up to the surface to form the crust. Eventually, gases from inside the Earth were released above the surface through volcanoes and formed the atmosphere around the Earth.

At first, the atmosphere did not shield the Earth from the Sun's ultraviolet rays. These rays, together with electricity from lightning, may have created complex patterns of chemicals in the oceans. Over time these became the earliest forms of life on the planet: one-celled organisms similar to today's bacteria. This probably happened about 3.8 billion years ago. By about 3 billion years ago, simple life forms had developed in the oceans.

▲ **Billions of years ago** gases from inside the Earth escaped to form a cloudy atmosphere. Rain fell to make oceans. Gradually, life formed in the oceans and added oxygen to the atmosphere.

The early atmosphere
Earth's early atmosphere consisted mostly of water vapour and carbon dioxide gas. Plants used carbon dioxide to make food and gave off oxygen gas as waste. Oxygen made the atmosphere breathable for animals. Gradually, more advanced forms of life developed, and eventually living creatures moved out of the sea on to the land, where they breathed air.

The atmosphere today is made up mainly of nitrogen, from the eruptions of volcanoes over billions of years, and the oxygen produced by plants.

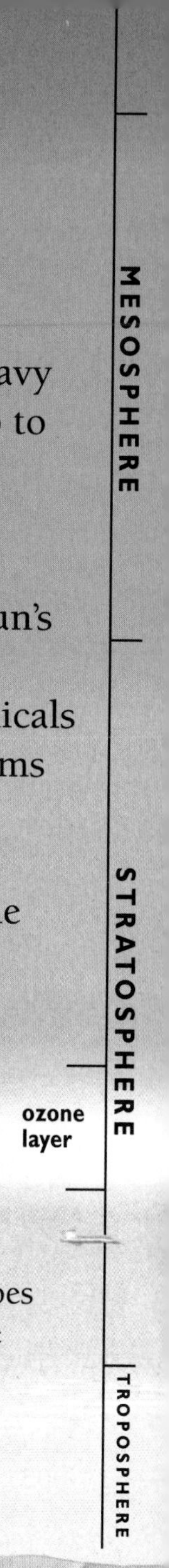

MESOSPHERE

STRATOSPHERE

ozone layer

TROPOSPHERE

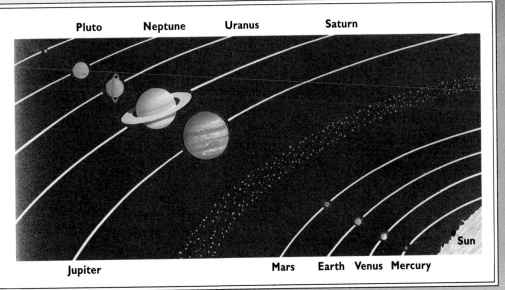

Pluto Neptune Uranus Saturn

Jupiter Mars Earth Venus Mercury Sun

The Earth is the right distance from the Sun to sustain life. It is neither too hot nor too cold for living things, and contains the mixture of gases and water they need to survive.

The other planets are probably too hot or too cold, or the gases in their atmospheres would kill living things. (However, scientists believe that simple life forms may have once existed on Mars.) Mercury is scorching hot by day and freezing at night; Venus has a thick atmosphere of poisonous carbon dioxide; Mars is bitterly cold, and the other planets are even colder than Mars.

Layers of atmosphere

The atmosphere consists of different layers. All living things and the weather are contained in the lowest layer, the troposphere. The stratosphere is like a lid on the troposphere, holding the weather near the Earth's surface. Gases in the atmosphere trap the Sun's heat. This keeps the planet about 15°C warmer than it would be otherwise.

When oxygen first became part of the atmosphere, it reacted with the Sun's ultraviolet rays to make ozone. A layer of ozone in the atmosphere acts as a shield, absorbing about 90 percent of the Sun's ultraviolet rays. These rays damage all living things, so without the ozone layer there would be no life on Earth.

nitrogen oxygen others

◀ **The atmosphere** today is made up of about 75 percent nitrogen and 23 percent oxygen, with traces of water vapour, argon and other gases such as carbon dioxide, helium, methane and krypton.

▶ **The layer of the atmosphere** in which we live, called the troposphere, forms only a tiny part of the whole atmosphere. It would only take you a few hours to walk up to the top of the troposphere. To walk to the top of the atmosphere and out into space would take several weeks.

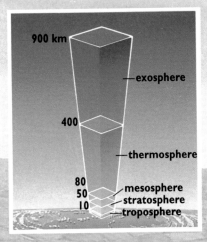

900 km

400

80
50
10

— exosphere

— thermosphere

— mesosphere
— stratosphere
— troposphere

Spinning Earth

The Earth beneath your feet may seem to be still, but it is spinning around like a top as it orbits the Sun. The Earth travels at a speed of more than 104,500 kilometres per hour, taking a year to orbit once around the Sun. The orbit covers about 940 million kilometres. It is the Earth's full spin every 24 hours that gives us day and night.

Seasons occur because the Earth leans slightly to one side in space. This affects the amount of light and heat that different parts of the Earth receive from the Sun on its yearly orbit.

▲ **A French physicist,** named Jean Foucault, used a pendulum to show the Earth's spin. When the pendulum was released, it swung along a marked line. After several hours, the pendulum seemed to have changed direction, but it was really the Earth below the pendulum that had turned.

Day and night

Although the Sun seems to rise in the sky during the day and sink at night, it is really the Earth that is moving, not the Sun.

When your part of the Earth turns toward the Sun, it looks as if the Sun is rising, and you have daytime. When your part of the Earth turns away from the Sun, the Sun seems to disappear below the horizon. No sunlight reaches your part of the Earth, so it gets dark and you have night.

On the other side of the world, people are having breakfast just as you are going to bed. For instance, when it is breakfast time in Britain, it is night in the United States. When it is evening in France, it is early morning in Japan.

day time

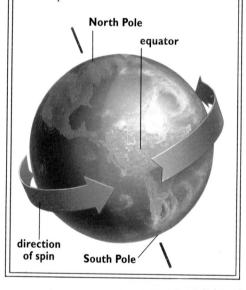

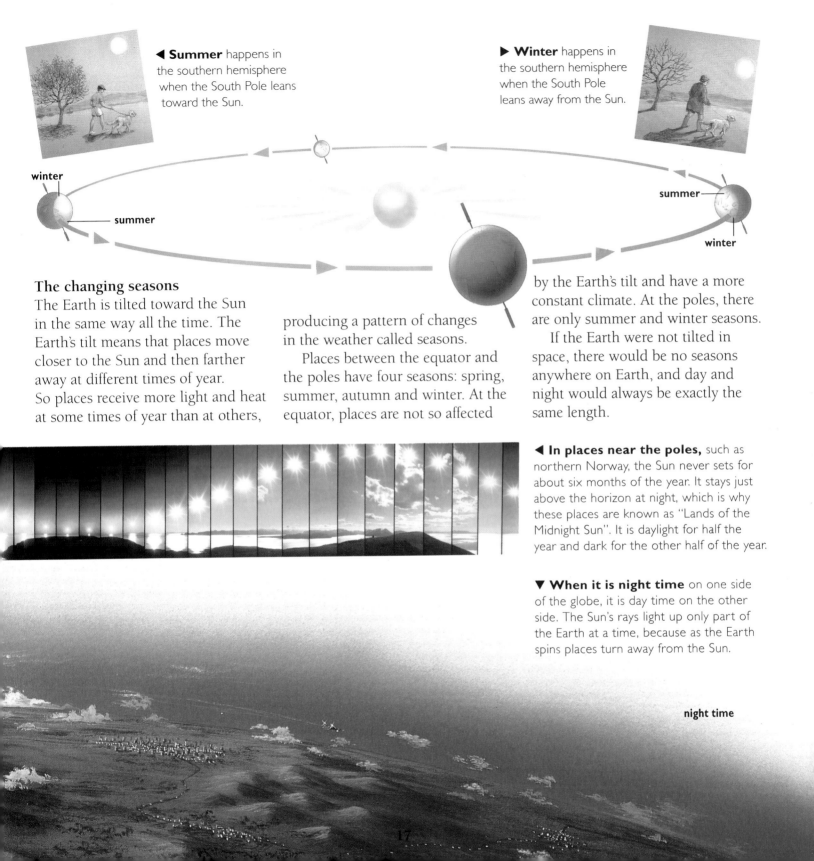

◄ **Summer** happens in the southern hemisphere when the South Pole leans toward the Sun.

▶ **Winter** happens in the southern hemisphere when the South Pole leans away from the Sun.

winter

summer

summer

winter

The changing seasons

The Earth is tilted toward the Sun in the same way all the time. The Earth's tilt means that places move closer to the Sun and then farther away at different times of year. So places receive more light and heat at some times of year than at others, producing a pattern of changes in the weather called seasons.

Places between the equator and the poles have four seasons: spring, summer, autumn and winter. At the equator, places are not so affected by the Earth's tilt and have a more constant climate. At the poles, there are only summer and winter seasons.

If the Earth were not tilted in space, there would be no seasons anywhere on Earth, and day and night would always be exactly the same length.

◄ **In places near the poles,** such as northern Norway, the Sun never sets for about six months of the year. It stays just above the horizon at night, which is why these places are known as "Lands of the Midnight Sun". It is daylight for half the year and dark for the other half of the year.

▼ **When it is night time** on one side of the globe, it is day time on the other side. The Sun's rays light up only part of the Earth at a time, because as the Earth spins places turn away from the Sun.

night time

FORCES FROM INSIDE THE EARTH

THE HEAT INSIDE THE EARTH IS THE DRIVING FORCE BEHIND the movement of rocks on the surface. It makes continents move around the globe, pushes up mountains and volcanoes, and causes earthquakes to happen.

The structure of the Earth

As we walk around on the Earth's surface, we are like ants crawling over an apple, unable to pierce the skin. Below the Earth's "skin", or crust, lie different layers that make up the mantle and core. Although we cannot take samples from the deeper layers, we can guess what they are made of by studying the Sun, other planets and meteorites. We know that the thin, outer crust is made of much lighter material than either the mantle or core.

▲ In 1996, the eruption of Mount Ruapehu on New Zealand's North Island sent a cloud of ash and steam 11 kilometres into the sky. The nearby town of Turangi was covered in ash and a dense cloud blocked out the Sun.

The crust
The Earth's crust is about 5 kilometres thick under the oceans, and about 35 kilometres thick under the continents. Under the biggest mountain ranges, the crust extends as far as 121 kilometres. The crust beneath the continents is much older than the crust under the oceans.

▶ The deepest hole people have ever drilled into the Earth reaches down 13 kilometres under the Kola Peninsula in Russia. Even the deepest hole only just scratches the Earth's surface!

drilling site

crust

mantle

crust

mantle

outer core

inner core

JOURNEY TO THE CENTRE OF THE EARTH

The distance from the Earth's surface to the centre is about 6,400 kilometres. The deepest anyone has ever been inside the Earth is just 4 kilometres down a mine in South Africa. If you could climb down a ladder to the middle of the Earth, at an average speed of about 3–4 kilometres per hour, it would take you about 10 weeks to get there, without stopping to rest! You could never really make a journey like this because it is far too hot, and the pressure inside the Earth would crush you to death.

The core and mantle

The Earth's core is made of dense material, probably the metals iron and nickel. It is extremely hot, with temperatures over 5,500°C. At these temperatures the metals should melt to liquid, but the core is pressed so hard by the weight of all the layers around it that it may be only partly liquid.

Scientists think that the outer core, which is mainly iron and nickel, is liquid, while the inner core, which is mainly iron, is solid. Sandwiched between the thin, light crust and the heavy core is the mantle. This makes up more than 80 percent of the Earth's volume and is about 3,000 kilometres thick. The mantle rock is so hot some of it has melted to form gooey molten rock, called magma. The slow movement of magma circling within the mantle makes the rocks on the surface move.

▶ **Magma rising** close to the surface may heat up water under the ground. This water may form hot springs on the Earth's surface, such as these at Rotorua, New Zealand.

▲ **In the middle** of the Earth is a hot iron core. Around this is the lighter, stony mantle, and around the edge is the thin crust.

Moving continents

The surface of the Earth is broken up into pieces, like the cracked shell of a boiled egg. There are about nine large pieces, or plates, and twelve smaller ones. Each plate consists of part of the crust and the top layer of the mantle.

The plates move a few centimetres every year, carrying the continents with them. This movement is known as continental drift. The plates slide about because of hot rocks churning round inside the mantle.

The study of the way the plates move is called plate tectonics.

▲ **The continents** were joined together millions of years ago and have drifted apart. They are still moving today. If you look at a map of the world, you will see that the shapes of the continents fit together, like the pieces of a jigsaw.

220 million years ago
At this time, all the continents were joined together in one giant continent called Pangaea – meaning "all Earth". Plants and animals could spread all over the world and climates were warmer than today. About 200 million years ago, Pangaea began to split into two parts: a northern section called Laurasia and a southern section called Gondwanaland.

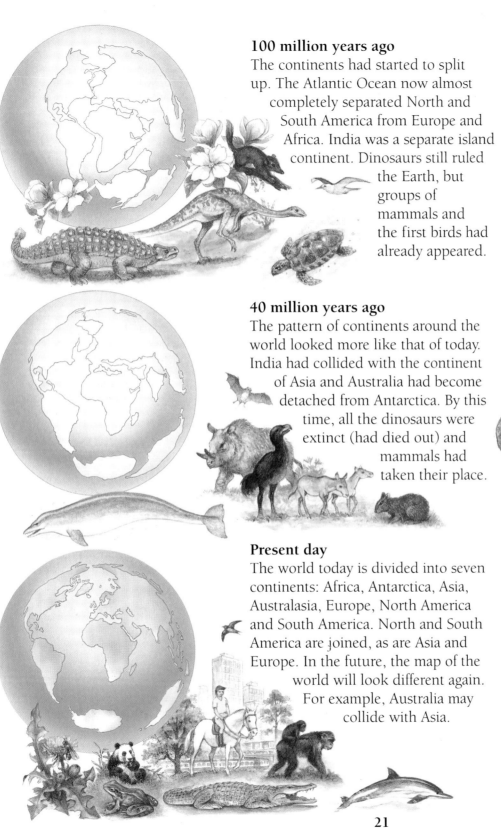

100 million years ago

The continents had started to split up. The Atlantic Ocean now almost completely separated North and South America from Europe and Africa. India was a separate island continent. Dinosaurs still ruled the Earth, but groups of mammals and the first birds had already appeared.

40 million years ago

The pattern of continents around the world looked more like that of today. India had collided with the continent of Asia and Australia had become detached from Antarctica. By this time, all the dinosaurs were extinct (had died out) and mammals had taken their place.

Present day

The world today is divided into seven continents: Africa, Antarctica, Asia, Australasia, Europe, North America and South America. North and South America are joined, as are Asia and Europe. In the future, the map of the world will look different again. For example, Australia may collide with Asia.

CLUES TO THE PAST

How do we know that the continents were once joined in one giant landmass? The answer lies in fossils and rocks.

The fossilised remains of many types of animals (for example, Lystrosaurus) and plants that lived about 220 million years ago have been found in several of today's continents. They could spread through the world because the land had not yet become divided up by the oceans.

If we fit the continents back together again, we also find that the same types of rocks lie on each side of the joins. The rocks became separated as the continents broke apart.

Lystrosaurus

▼ **Fossils are the remains** of living things that have been preserved in rock, sometimes for millions of years. Only a fraction of life on Earth is ever fossilised. To be preserved, a living thing must be buried quickly before its body is eaten, rots away or is broken. Fossils are often found in sedimentary rocks, formed from layers of sand, mud and clay, which all provide ideal conditions for the formation of fossils.

fossil ammonite

Where plates meet

▲ **A rift valley occurs** where a crack between two plates is pulling the plates apart. The African Rift Valley runs down eastern Africa from the Red Sea to Mozambique. Earthquakes and active volcanoes in the area show that the plates are still moving apart. In the future, a new ocean may separate eastern Africa from the rest of the continent.

Where two of the Earth's crustal plates meet, they may collide together, slide past each other or move apart. At some plate boundaries, a mixture of all three movements takes place. Each plate grows at one of its edges as new material rises up from inside the Earth. The other edge of each plate is gradually destroyed, either by sliding down inside the Earth, or by being pushed up into mountain ranges.

Although the plates move only a few centimetres a year, they cover thousands of kilometres over millions of years. As they collide and separate, they continually change the face of the globe.

▶ **When two plates** slide past each other, they cause cracks in the rock, called faults. Earthquakes occur at fault lines (see *page 30*).

▶ **Most plates** move apart beneath the oceans. The edges of the plates occur at the top of mountain ranges called mid-oceanic ridges. These ridges may be thousands of kilometres long.

▶ **Hot rock** churning in the mantle moves the plates in the crust.

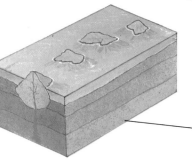

▲ **A chain of volcanoes** has formed the islands of Hawaii above an intensely hot area, called a hot spot, in the middle of an oceanic plate. The volcanoes occur where magma has burned its way right through the plate on to the surface.

THE WORLD'S PLATE BOUNDARIES

This map shows the edges, or boundaries, between the plates that make up the Earth's crust. As you can see, most boundaries are under the oceans, although some are quite close to the edges of continents.

Most of the plates include some ocean and some continent – for instance, the South American plate includes half of the South Atlantic Ocean as well as the continent of South America.

Volcanoes and earthquakes usually occur at plate boundaries where the crust is weak. They are evidence that the crust is moving.

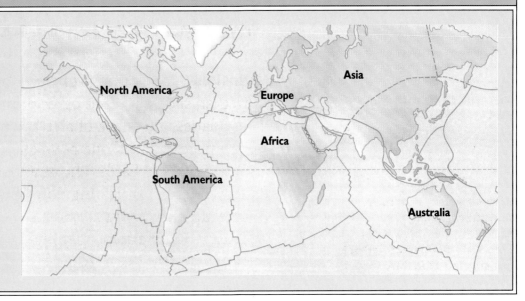

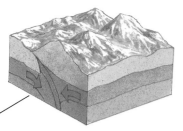

▲ **When two plates** move toward each other, the edges of the plates may crumple up into mountain ranges. The Alps and the Himalayas were both formed this way.

▲ **Deep ocean trenches,** such as the Japan Trench, form when two plates collide, forcing one plate down inside the Earth's crust.

Colliding plates

When an oceanic plate collides with a continental plate, the less dense continental plate will ride above the denser oceanic plate. The oceanic plate is forced down into the mantle in a process called subduction. This is happening in several places around the world, such as the Marianas Trench in the Pacific Ocean (*see page 25*).

As it sinks deeper into the Earth, the oceanic plate is gradually destroyed because it gets so hot that it melts and becomes magma (*see page 19*). Magma is less dense than the solid rock above it because it is mixed with gases. It either works its way upward on to the surface to form volcanoes, or it cools down, becomes heavier and forms rocks within the Earth's crust.

Separating plates

Most plates move apart beneath the oceans. Magma from the mantle wells up through the crest of a mid-ocean ridge (*see page 24*) and becomes solid as it cools down, forming a new sea floor. As the ridge pulls apart again and new cracks appear, more magma rises to fill the gaps, creating even more sea floor.

This process is called sea-floor spreading. The sea floor is like a conveyor belt for material rising from the mantle and returning down into the mantle again. Some oceans, such as the Pacific Ocean, are shrinking, while others, such as the Atlantic, are growing bigger. This means the overall size of the Earth's crust stays the same.

The movement of all the plates is driven by the movement of hot rocks in the mantle (*see page 19*).

23

Under the ocean

Planet Earth could also be called Planet Water, because over two-thirds of the surface is covered by sea water. Beneath this salty water, the Earth's crust rises up and down, just as it does on land, creating mountains, valleys, canyons and plains. The tallest mountain, the biggest waterfall, the deepest trench and the longest mountain range on Earth are all found under the oceans.

Most oceans are less than 200 million years old and were formed after the supercontinent Pangaea broke up to form the separate continents in the world today.

▲ **Until recently,** the undersea world was as much a mystery as the planets in space. Today, people use deep diving submersibles (like the one above), undersea robots and remote sensing equipment, such as SONAR, to gather information.

▼ **Just like on land,** the landscape under the sea is shaped by the movement of the plates which make up the Earth's crust.

continental shelf

ocean trench

abyssal plain

seamount

mid-ocean ridge

Ocean floor features

The edges of the continents slope down under the ocean to form continental shelves. A continental shelf may vary from a few kilometres to about 480 kilometres or more in width. The water is less than 200 metres deep; beyond the shelf, the ocean floor drops away to depths of 2,000–4,000 metres. Valleys called submarine canyons cut into some continental shelves, making a path to the deep ocean floor.

Most of the ocean floor, between the continental shelves and the mid-ocean ridges, consists of wide, flat

24

◀ **Some islands** in the oceans are really the tops of undersea volcanoes rising from the ocean floor.

Volcanic island arc

BLACK SMOKERS

Hot, mineral-rich water sometimes gushes up from cracks, called vents, in the seabed, forming stacks up to 9 metres tall. Sulphur from these vents turns the water black, so the stacks have been named "black smokers".

Unusual creatures, such as giant tube worms and giant clams, live around the vents. As no light reaches the vents for green plants to provide food for these animals, they get energy from the sulphur, on which the bacteria in their bodies feed.

areas known as abyssal plains. They have an average depth of about 4,000 metres and are the flattest features on Earth. Abyssal plains develop where sediment builds up enough to cover the hills and valleys on the ocean floor. This sediment is called ooze. Some ooze comes from the remains of ocean creatures and some from volcanic ash, deep-sea vents, rivers or melting icebergs.

Where the plates of the Earth's crust collide, deep ocean trenches may form. They are often 8–10 kilometres deep, over 950 kilometres wide and thousands of kilometres long. Sediment builds up in the trenches as rivers carry sand, mud and silt off the land and deposit them under the ocean. Earthquakes and volcanoes are common in ocean trenches because of the moving crust.

Undersea mountains that do not reach above sea level are called seamounts. Most are cone shaped, often with steeply sloping sides; those with flattened tops are called guyots. The largest seamount is in the Atlantic Ocean. It is 4,000 metres high and about 100 kilometres wide.

◀ **In 1960,** two scientists in a submersible reached the bottom of the Marianas Trench, in the Pacific Ocean, just west of the Philippines. At over 11 kilometres deep, it is the deepest ocean trench. If the highest mountain on the surface, Mount Everest, was put into the Marianas Trench, its top would still be far below sea level. The Marianas Trench is also the second-longest trench in the world, stretching for 2,400 kilometres.

Mount Everest

Marianas Trench

Exploding Earth

When hot, molten rock and gases from inside the earth escape through cracks in the crust, volcanoes erupt on the surface. This often happens at the edges of the Earth's crustal plates (*see page 20*), although with hot-spot volcanoes, such as those on Hawaii, lava bursts through the middle of a plate.

Volcanoes are like safety valves in the Earth's crust, releasing the built-up pressure caused by gases below the surface. The explosion of a volcano is similar to a can of fizzy drink being opened: in both cases the escaping bubbles of gas cause the liquid to explode.

▶ **When magma pours out** on to the Earth's surface, it is called lava. Layers of lava build up, cool down and harden to form a mountain of rock.

crater

side vent

lava flow

old magma chamber

new magma chamber

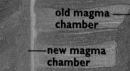

Active, dormant or extinct

A volcano that may erupt at any moment is called an active volcano. There are about 1,300 of these in the world at the moment, but only between 20 and 30 erupt each year. Japan has 10 percent of the world's active volcanoes. Others, such as Mount Rainier in Washington State, U.S.A, are "sleeping", or dormant. They have been quiet for many years, but may erupt in the future. If a volcano is unlikely ever to erupt again, it is called extinct. Mount Kilimanjaro in Africa is an extinct volcano.

Buried alive

A volcanic eruption flings boiling hot rocks and clouds of ash and steam into the air. The steam and ash may mix to form thick mud, which buries everything in its path.

▶ **A volcano's shape depends** on the type of lava and how far it flows, as well as on the strength of the eruption. Runny lava makes shield-shaped volcanoes, while thicker lava makes dome-shaped layers.

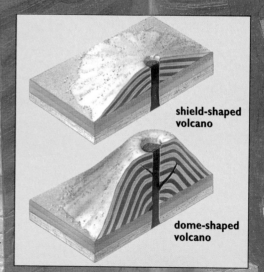

shield-shaped volcano

dome-shaped volcano

Lethal lava

The violence of an eruption depends on the amount of gas in the lava and magma, and how easily it escapes. Thick lava with a lot of trapped gas causes violent eruptions. It may even cause a volcano to blow its top, leaving a large crater called a caldera. This happened in Washington State on Mount St. Helens in May 1980. Lava is very hot, up to 1,200°C. As lava cools down, its surface hardens into a rough skin if it is thick, and a smooth skin if it is runny. Smooth-skinned lava is called "pahoehoe" and rough-skinned lava is called "aa", which are Hawaiian words. As it hardens, it may crack to form six-sided columns. Lava erupting under the sea is called pillow lava because it forms pillow-shaped lumps.

pumice

basalt

rhyolite

obsidian

▲ **Most volcanic rocks** contain the mineral silica, although runny lavas contain less than thicker lavas. The type of rock that forms depends on the minerals and gas in the lava, as well as how quickly the lava cools down. Obsidian is smooth because it cools so fast crystals cannot form.

FAMOUS ERUPTIONS

About 3,500 years ago, the ancient Greek island of Thera (present-day Santorini) was the site of a huge explosion that spread ash over the eastern Mediterranean area.

In A.D. 79, a massive explosion blew off the top of Mount Vesuvius in Italy, burying the city of Pompeii under 6 metres of ash. More than 20,000 people died, and the hardened ash preserved the shapes of their bodies, as well as the buildings.

In 1883, the volcanic island of Krakatoa in Indonesia exploded, throwing ash and lava 80 kilometres into the sky and causing a huge tidal wave that killed thousands of people.

shapes of bodies preserved in volcanic ash at Pompeii

Volcanic rocks

When lava cools down, it forms igneous rocks, meaning "fire" rocks. Some igneous rocks contain valuable ores and minerals, such as diamonds, gold and copper. Lavas that flow easily tend to form dark rocks, such as basalt. Thicker lavas form rocks, such as rhyolite, which are lighter in colour because they contain a lot of the mineral silica. If gas is trapped in thick lava, it hardens into a frothy rock called pumice. Pumice is full of air spaces and is so light that it is the only rock that floats on water. Granite contains a lot of crystals because it forms when magma cools slowly, giving the crystals time to form.

▶ **A spectacular stream of** red-hot lava flows from a volcano in northeastern Zaire. This volcano is called Kimanura.

Volcanic landscapes

A volcano rising from the Earth's surface is the most obvious sign that an area is volcanic. However, hot magma under the ground changes rocks and water in the Earth's crust to produce many other features. Some, such as hot water springs, appear on the surface. Other features, such as bands or domes of rock, form under the ground when magma cools below the surface. Eventually, the forces of weathering and erosion (*see page 10*) may wear away the overlying rock, so that the hard volcanic rocks are exposed. Another feature of volcanic landscapes is lush vegetation populated by humans because of the rich soils and abundance of minerals.

▲ In the high mountains of northern Japan, macaque monkeys often bathe in hot springs to keep warm during the cold winter months. The water is heated by rocks beneath the Earth's surface.

Underground features

Much of the molten magma that bubbles up toward the Earth's surface stays trapped under the ground, where it pushes its way into the rocks and cools slowly to form igneous rocks, such as granite and rhyolite. These new rocks, called igneous intrusions, may follow lines of weakness in the rock if the magma is runny, or they may break across the layers of the rocks if the magma is thicker and stronger.

The largest igneous intrusions are called batholiths. Each one is at least 100 square kilometres in area. The largest batholith in North America is 1,500 kilometres long.

Magma that forces its way through a layer of rock may spread out into a dome shape with a flat base, called a laccolith. Where magma has pushed its way between layers of rock to make horizontal sheets, it forms igneous intrusions called sills.

Vertical intrusions that cut through the rocks to form walls of volcanic rock are called dikes. Large numbers of dikes tend to spread out from batholiths.

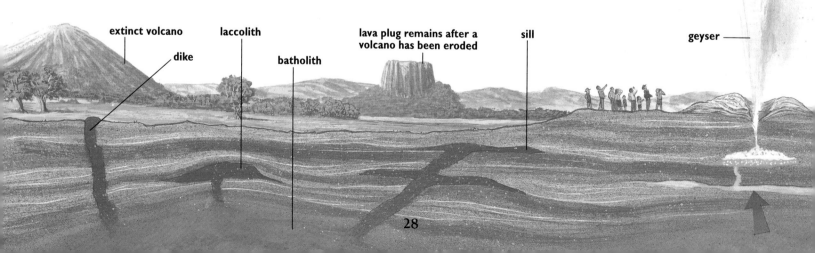

extinct volcano   laccolith   lava plug remains after a volcano has been eroded   sill   geyser

dike   batholith

Useful volcanoes

Volcanic soils are rich and fertile, and in places such as Indonesia, people farm the land on the lower slopes of volcanoes. Countries such as Iceland, New Zealand and Japan use volcanic energy to provide people with heat and power. Sulphur deposits that form near volcanoes are used in explosives and fertilisers, and are useful for making rubber heat resistant and last longer. Volcanic rocks such as basalt and granite make strong building materials.

steam goes up pipe to make electricity

turbine

generator

cold water pumped down

water seeps through cracks in hot rocks and turns to steam

▼ **Different types of hot water** features can be found in volcanic areas. Geysers are springs which send out large fountains of water and steam every so often. Small vents that shoot out steam and gas are called fumaroles. Mud pools form where water and volcanic gases turn the rocks into boiling hot mud.

▲ **The underground** heat in volcanic areas can be harnessed to provide geothermal energy. The heat turns water in the rocks into steam. The force of the steam then turns the blades of a turbine that generates electricity.

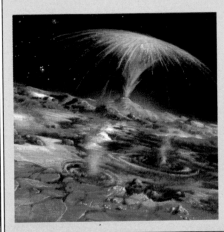

heat rising from magma

mud pool

fumarole

water under the ground

hot springs

mineral deposits

Earthquakes

An earthquake is a trembling or shaking of the ground caused by a sudden release of energy stored in rocks beneath the Earth's surface. Earthquakes happen where the crust is weak, and where there is a build-up of pressure under the ground caused by plate movements (*see page 20*). As the pressure is suddenly released, the rocks crack or shudder past each other, sending out vibrations that make the ground shake. These vibrations, known as seismic waves, spread out from an underground point called the focus. The force of the waves depends on the depth of the focus, the strength of the surrounding rocks and how much they move. Every year there is a total of about 500,000 earthquakes.

▲ **A huge earthquake** hit Mexico in 1985. The unstable layers of sand and mud, on which Mexico City is built, shook like jelly. The town of Acapulco, which stands on solid rock, was not badly damaged.

Earthquake waves

Two main types of wave radiate from an earthquake's focus. Body waves travel inside the Earth, spreading out in all directions. Surface waves travel on the Earth's surface away from the epicentre, the point on the surface directly above the focus.

Surface waves tend to cause more damage to property than body waves because they produce more ground movement and travel more slowly. The surface waves from a huge earthquake in Alaska were strong enough to force water to spill out of swimming pools thousands of kilometres away in southern U.S.A.

There are two types of body waves: primary (P) waves and secondary (S) waves. P-waves stretch and squeeze the rocks, like a wire spring being pulled back and forth.

They travel very fast, at 5 kilometres per second, and are the first to arrive after a quake. P-waves do not spread out evenly, but spread strongly in four directions.

S-waves are much slower. They travel at 3 kilometres per second and move the rocks up and down or from side to side.

Waves from very large earthquakes are so powerful that they can echo round and round inside the Earth for a day or more.

▼ **Buildings can be designed to** withstand earthquakes. Strong foundations are important, and a tapering shape at the top of a skyscraper makes it more stable. Sensors and computers can control the way a building moves during a quake, so that it sways with the Earth's vibrations.

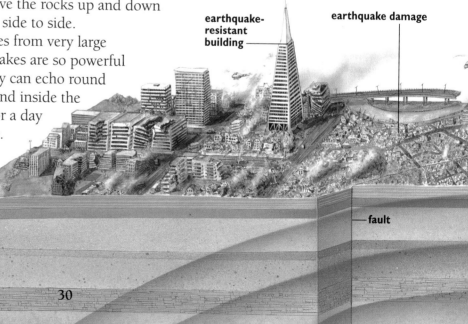

earthquake-resistant building

earthquake damage

fault

Detecting earthquakes

It is hard to predict when earthquakes will occur, although there may be a series of small shocks before a big quake, and animals may become restless if they sense the vibrations. The first instrument for detecting earthquakes was invented in A.D. 130 by Zhang Heng, a Chinese astronomer. It consisted of bronze balls balanced on the sides of a jar, which fell down if the Earth shook.

Nowadays, an instrument called a seismometer is used. A needle on a scale responds to the shaking of the ground. Then the seismometer produces a permanent record of the movements, drawn as a line on a moving strip of paper.

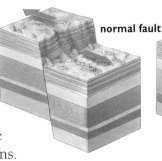
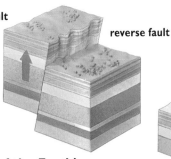

▲ As the plates of the Earth's crust jostle each other, they often make cracks called faults in the rock. Faults usually happen along lines of weakness in the rock. In a normal fault, a block of rock slips down as the crust is pulled apart. In a reverse fault, a block of rock is pushed up above another as the crust is squeezed or compressed. In a tear fault, blocks of rock slide past each other in opposite directions.

▶ Vibrations from an earthquake start at the focus and radiate out in concentric circles, like the ripples from a stone thrown into a pond. The vibrations may be felt as far as 400 km away. The nearer the focus is to the surface, the greater the damage tends to be. The devastation is greatest at the epicentre.

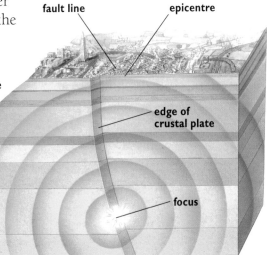

fault line

epicentre

edge of crustal plate

focus

epicentre

EARTHQUAKE SCALES

The size of earthquakes is measured on two scales. The Mercalli Scale (below) measures how much and what kind of damage the earthquake has caused. The Richter Scale measures the amount of energy released by the quake.

The Mercalli Scale

1	Slightly felt	
2–3	Felt by a few people, hanging objects swing	
4–5	Objects rattle and fall over, liquids spill	
6–7	Felt by everyone, hard to stand, windows break, buildings damaged	
8–9	Towers and chimneys collapse, cracks appear in ground	
10–11	Severe damage to buildings and bridges, railroad tracks bend, underground pipes break	
12	Nearly everything is damaged, large areas of land slip and move	

▲ **Fossils of sea creatures** are sometimes found on mountains, such as the Himalayas, whose rocks were once under the ocean. The rocks were pushed to the surface by forces inside the Earth.

Mountain building

Most of the world's great mountain ranges have been pushed up by movements of the Earth's plates (*see page 22*). There are three main types of mountains: fold mountains, such as the Andes in South America, volcanic mountains such as Mount Kilimanjaro in Africa, and block mountains, such as the Sierra Nevada in North America. Fold mountains form where plates crash together, causing the rocks to buckle upward into folds. Volcanic mountains build up when magma wells up on to the Earth's surface. Block mountains form when pressure from beneath the surface cracks the crust into blocks, which move up and down, causing fault lines (*see page 31*). Mountain building takes millions of years.

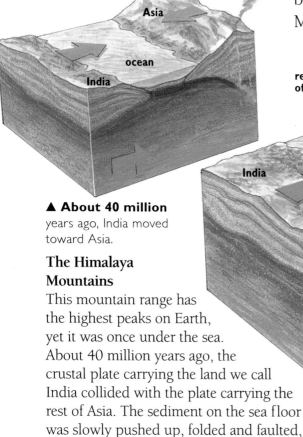

▲ **About 40 million** years ago, India moved toward Asia.

The Himalaya Mountains

This mountain range has the highest peaks on Earth, yet it was once under the sea. About 40 million years ago, the crustal plate carrying the land we call India collided with the plate carrying the rest of Asia. The sediment on the sea floor was slowly pushed up, folded and faulted, to make the Himalaya Mountain chain.

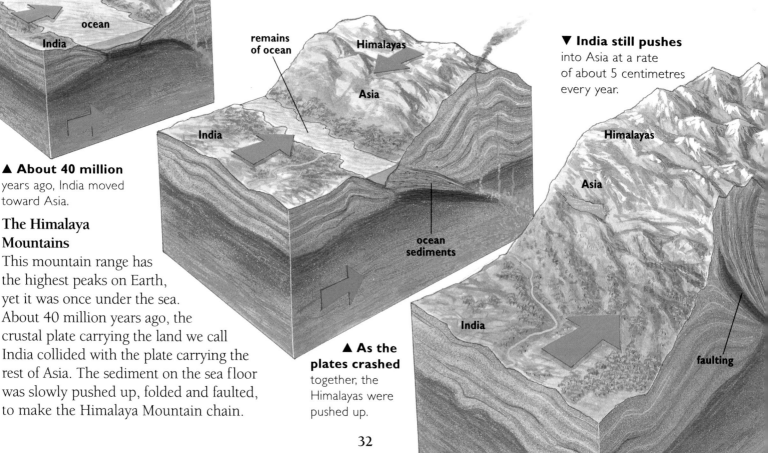

▲ **As the plates crashed** together, the Himalayas were pushed up.

▼ **India still pushes** into Asia at a rate of about 5 centimetres every year.

TYPES OF FOLDING

Folds usually happen where layers of rock are crumpled up and bent as they are squeezed by forces inside the Earth, like someone pushing layers of blankets up or bending them down.

Depending on the amount of pressure, folds can be all sorts of shapes. Some folds are very simple, while those under more pressure overturn, break off or pile on top of one another. Folds may also have faults cutting through them.

◄ An anticline happens when folds form an arch, from a few metres to many kilometres high.

► A syncline is where folds form a trough or a basin, such as the London basin.

◄ Overfolds happen when one side of an anticline is forced over another.

► Recumbent folds are where the sides of a fold are pushed over so much they are almost horizontal.

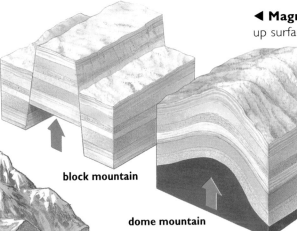

block mountain

dome mountain

folding

◄ Magma rising to the surface can push up surface rocks to form dome mountains. Block mountains form when blocks of land are faulted and pushed up.

Evolution of mountains

Mountains are usually found in chains, or ridges, that may extend for thousands of kilometres but are only a few hundred kilometres wide.

There are three stages in the development of a typical mountain chain. First, sediment is washed off the land by rivers, or thrown out by volcanoes. The sediment builds up in thick layers, usually under the sea. Second, the rocks are folded and faulted into new shapes. Third, there is a period of uplift – when the rocks are forced upward – and erosion, which lasts for many millions of years.

If uplift is greater than erosion, the mountains will continue to grow upward. Eventually, erosion takes over, and the mountains are worn down to a flat plain and become part of the level interior of a continent.

Under pressure

Rocks are under such pressure during mountain building that they become compressed. The rocks that formed the Alps, for instance, are estimated to have covered an area of ocean floor 480 kilometres wide and became squashed to form a range of mountains just 200 kilometres wide.

▼ When mountains are made, rocks are changed by heat and pressure to form new rocks, called metamorphic rocks. The marble being cut from this quarry in Carrara, Italy, is a type of metamorphic rock formed from limestone.

Mountain life

The range of climates, habitats and wildlife concentrated on a mountain can make travelling to the top seem like a journey from the equator to the poles. Habitats range from forests lower down to grasslands, rock and snow on the higher slopes. Mountain wildlife has to adapt to the thin air at high altitudes, as well as strong winds up to 320 kilometres per hour, biting cold and intense sunlight. Some animals cope by migrating up and down the mountain with the changing seasons.

All mountains are divided into broad zones, each with its own typical plants and animals. The diagram on this page shows the zones of the Rocky Mountains, which stretch for 4,800 kilometres down western North America.

▲ **This satellite photo** taken from space clearly shows the snowy peaks of the Austrian Alps, in south-central Europe. These fold mountains (*see page 32*) cover more than 207,200 square kilometres and have many peaks over 3,000 metres.

Vegetation and climate

The vegetation changes as you go higher up a mountain slope because the temperature falls about 0.5°C for every 100 metres you climb.

On the lower slopes, there are deciduous forests. Deciduous trees lose their leaves in winter. Higher up, there are forests of evergreen trees that do not lose their leaves and can withstand the cold and the weight of snow on their branches. Trees cannot grow above a certain height, called

the tree line, because it is too cold and windy. Above the tree line, there are only shrubs, grasses and small, low-growing plants.

Above a certain height, called the snow line, there is always snow on the ground. The snow line is at sea level at the poles, but rises to 5,000 metres in the tropics, near the equator.

above the tree line is alpine tundra – an area where grasses, mosses, lichens and small flowering plants grow

subalpine forest is mostly coniferous trees, including lodgepole pine, western red cedar and white spruce

forests higher up contain deciduous trees, such as aspen, and evergreens, including yellow pine and douglas fir

deciduous trees grow on lower slopes, where they are close to water sources

▼ **The vegetation zones** of the Rocky Mountains range from deciduous forests on the lower slopes to coniferous forests higher up. Above the tree line, there are grassy meadows, with bare rocky slopes beneath the snow peaks.

▲ **Deserts occur** on the eastern side of the Rocky Mountains in the rain shadow.

moist air drops rain on the western side of the Rockies

warm, dry air flows down the eastern side of the Rockies, leaving lower plains parched and dry – an effect called a "rain shadow"

▶ **An ibex** has hooves with narrow edges to dig into cracks, and hollow soles to cling to slopes.

▶ **An ibex's two toes** spread out when it lands to help it balance.

Plant adaptation

Plants at high altitudes are compact, to keep out wind and to trap warm air near the ground. They may have thick, hairy leaves to protect them from the Sun's strong rays. Many plants store water in their leaves as rain drains quickly through the thin soil.

Animal adaptation

Some mountain animals have developed extra-large hearts and lungs to help them get enough oxygen from the thin air. To survive the cold, animals such as yaks have thick coats. Some animals hibernate during winter, while those that do not may have coats that turn white for camouflage against the snow.

Only a few hardy insects can survive on mountaintops. They eat plants, and other insects swept up the mountain by strong winds.

◀ **On mountain tops,** the air pressure is half that at sea level. Mountain climbers usually carry breathing apparatus to give them more oxygen and help them to breathe.

HIGHEST MOUNTAINS

Many of the highest mountains in the world are in the Himalayan range, which stretches across parts of China, India, Tibet and Nepal. The highest of all, Mount Everest, was first climbed in 1953 by Edmund Hillary and Tenzing Norgay. The chart below shows the height of some of the world's highest mountains, and one of the world's tallest structures – the CN Tower – which looks tiny by comparison.

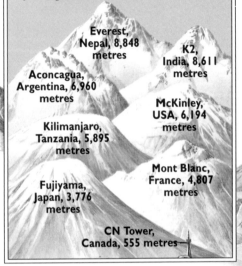

Everest, Nepal, 8,848 metres

K2, India, 8,611 metres

Aconcagua, Argentina, 6,960 metres

McKinley, USA, 6,194 metres

Kilimanjaro, Tanzania, 5,895 metres

Mont Blanc, France, 4,807 metres

Fujiyama, Japan, 3,776 metres

CN Tower, Canada, 555 metres

Mountain winds

When air meets a mountain range, it rises and cools. The water vapour in the air condenses into droplets of liquid water, which join up to form clouds. This is why the tops of mountains are often in the clouds and why they are usually rainy or snowy places.

Once the air has dropped most of its moisture on the top of a mountain, it flows down the other side as a dry wind.

WEATHER AND CLIMATE

THE SUN'S HEAT MAKES AIR AND WATER MOVE around the globe and causes our weather. The typical weather of an area over a long period of time is called the climate.

Climate zones

The Earth has three main climate zones, according to how far a place is from the equator. These zones are the cold polar regions, the hot tropics near the equator and the warm temperate areas in between.

The main climate zones can be further divided according to other things that affect temperature, such as the height of the land and its distance from the sea or mountains. The higher the land, the lower the temperature, while the sea keeps coastal areas warmer in winter and cooler in summer.

▲ **The Sun's rays hit** different places on Earth at different angles because the Earth is curved. The equator is heated more than the poles because the Sun's rays hit the equator directly.

Sun's rays

▼ **The ability of a surface** to reflect the Sun's energy is called its albedo. Snow and ice have an albedo of 90 percent, since they reflect back most of the Sun's heat. Asphalt roads reflect only 5 percent of the Sun's heat and absorb the rest.

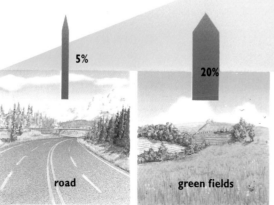
5%

20%

45%

90%

road

green fields

desert

snow and ice

▲ **This Tuareg man's** clothes help to protect him from the extreme temperatures in the Sahara Desert, Africa.

Different climates

Near the equator, the Sun's rays shine straight down and are concentrated on a relatively small area, giving these areas a hot climate. Equatorial areas are also very wet because the hot air rises and cools, forming clouds and rain. The atmosphere is humid, and it may rain every day. Desert climates occur in areas of warm, dry air (*see page 46*).

Farther from the equator, and in mountainous regions, places receive less heat from the Sun, so they are colder. At the poles, the large areas of snow and ice reflect most of the Sun's heat, which makes these areas colder still.

Temperate climates are found between the equator and the poles in places such as Europe, and parts of Australia and the U.S.A. They have warm summers, cold winters and rain all year round.

City climates

Cities tend to be warmer than the countryside because buildings and pollutants in the air hold in the Sun's heat longer than plants do. Artificial heating in offices and homes also increases the temperatures in cities. Large buildings block the winds that would otherwise blow away warm air. Cities can be up to 5°C warmer than the countryside and are often enclosed by a "heat island" of warm air which extends up to about 120 metres above street level.

▼ **Each of the Earth's climate zones** has its own typical plants and animals. The greatest variety occurs in the tropical rainforests. By contrast, only a few specially adapted creatures and plants can survive in the harsh polar and tundra regions.

polar and tundra
cold and dry all year

cold forest
cold winter;
warm summer

mountain
snow higher up; warm
and wet lower down

tropical rainforest
hot and wet all year

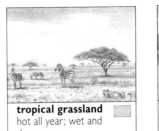

tropical grassland
hot all year; wet and
dry seasons

mediterranean
mild winter;
warm summer

temperate
mild and rainy all year

desert
hot and dry all year

dry grassland
hot, dry summer;
snowy winter

The world's winds

Wind is air moving from place to place around the Earth. This happens when air warms up or cools down. Over the whole globe, air always moves from warm areas to cooler ones. This is why warm air rises at the equator and moves toward the poles. Cold air moves the opposite way, from cold areas to warmer ones.

Three circles of wind blowing around the globe in each hemisphere create different wind patterns. The Earth's spin bends these winds to the right in the northern hemisphere and to the left in the southern hemisphere. This is called the Coriolis effect, which also affects ocean currents.

cold water flows toward the equator

30° north

equator

warm water flows away from the equator

30° south

High and low pressure

Warm air rises because it is "lighter" or less dense than cold air. It spreads out, so the particles in the air are farther apart, creating an area of low pressure called a depression or a low.

Cool air is "heavier" or more dense because the particles are closer together. It sinks down, pressing hard on the ground to create an area of high pressure called an anticyclone or a high.

Highs and lows bring different types of weather. Highs bring hot, dry weather in summer and cold, clear weather in winter. Lows bring unsettled weather, with clouds, rain or snow.

Winds are created when air moves from an area of high pressure to an area of low pressure – like air rushing out of a punctured bicycle tyre.

▶ **The Sun warms** air on the equator, making warm air and warm ocean currents that flow northward and southward from the equator. Farther from the equator, where the Sun has less heating power, the air and water cool down, sink and flow back toward the equator.

▼ **Strong, westerly winds** called jet streams blow between 10–16 kilometres above the Earth. They influence the weather in the atmosphere below them. The jet stream clouds in this picture are above Egypt

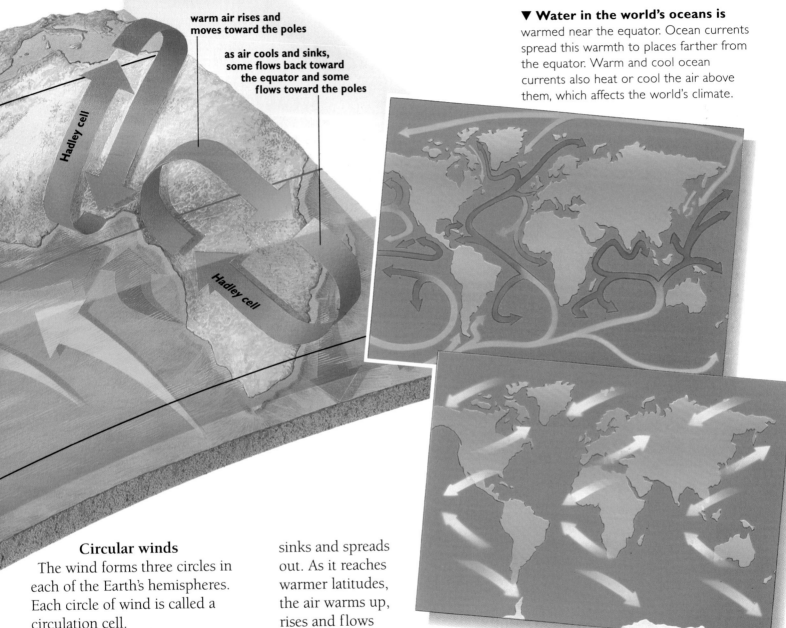

warm air rises and
moves toward the poles

as air cools and sinks,
some flows back toward
the equator and some
flows toward the poles

Hadley cell

Hadley cell

▼ Water in the world's oceans is warmed near the equator. Ocean currents spread this warmth to places farther from the equator. Warm and cool ocean currents also heat or cool the air above them, which affects the world's climate.

Circular winds

The wind forms three circles in each of the Earth's hemispheres. Each circle of wind is called a circulation cell.

On each side of the equator there is a circulation cell called a Hadley cell. Air rises at the equator, blows north or south, and sinks down again long before it reaches the poles and flows back to the equator.

At the poles, cold air in a second circle of winds, called a Polar cell, sinks and spreads out. As it reaches warmer latitudes, the air warms up, rises and flows back to the poles.

In between the Hadley cells and the Polar cells is a third circle of winds, called a Ferrel cell. In a Ferrel cell, air sinks down where it meets the Hadley cell and flows toward the poles, where it rises again as it meets the Polar cell.

▲ Near the Earth's surface, winds are divided into three belts: the trade winds of the tropics blowing toward the equator, the westerly winds of the middle latitudes and the easterly winds of the polar regions. The westerlies and easterlies are named for the directions from which they come.

Air masses and fronts

▲ **In parts of Asia** there are monsoon winds that blow in opposite directions at different times of year. In summer, the land's heat causes air to rise, drawing warm, moist air from over the oceans, bringing heavy rain and floods.

▼ **Land and sea breezes** are local coastal winds. During the day, the land heats up faster than the sea, so air rises from the land and a cool breeze blows from the sea to replace the rising air. At night, the land cools faster than the sea, so the wind blows in the opposite direction – off the land and on to the sea.

DAY

breeze blows from sea to land

land

sea

NIGHT

breeze blows from land to sea

land

sea

The Earth's atmosphere works as a giant heat "engine" (*see page 8*), moving heat from the equator to the poles to even out the differences in temperature. However, parts of the atmosphere, called air masses, may stay in one area for days or weeks, before being moved on by winds. Air masses take on the temperature and moisture of the Earth's surface beneath them and bring settled weather. But where one air mass meets another, stormy, changeable weather occurs at the edges, called fronts.

cumulonimbus cloud

cold air

heavy rain

cold front

warm wind

warm front

Types of air mass

There are two main types of air mass: polar and tropical. Air masses are also grouped according to whether they form over the land or the sea. Polar continental air masses form over cold land such as northern Canada; polar maritime air masses form over cold northern seas, such as the Arctic Ocean; tropical continental air masses start over warm, inland areas such as the Sahara Desert; and tropical maritime air masses come from oceans near the equator.

Fronts occur at the borders between air masses. Fronts are like battlefield front lines, where one air mass tries to move another out of the way. Tropical and polar air masses meet in temperate zones, where they form a line called the polar front. This front causes frequent changes in the weather. Depressions (*see page 38*) develop along the polar front, where a cold air mass chases a warm air mass, and creates a system of spiralling winds.

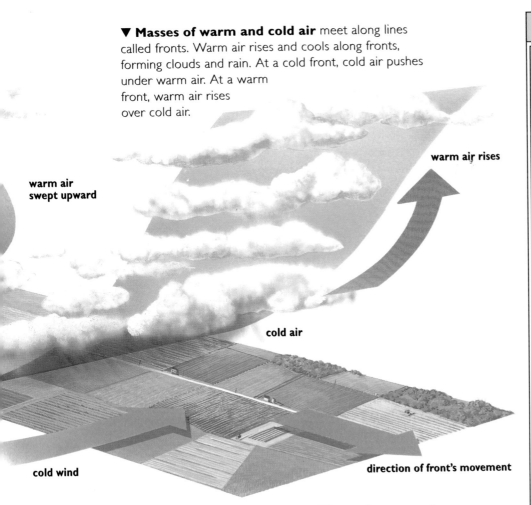

▼ **Masses of warm and cold air** meet along lines called fronts. Warm air rises and cools along fronts, forming clouds and rain. At a cold front, cold air pushes under warm air. At a warm front, warm air rises over cold air.

warm air rises

warm air swept upward

cold air

cold wind

direction of front's movement

Warm and cold fronts

In a warm front, a warm, moist, light air mass from the tropics rises over a cold, dry, heavier air mass from the poles. As it rises, the water vapour in the warm air cools and condenses into liquid water, forming clouds and rain along the gently sloping edge of the front.

In a cold front, a mass of cold air is forced under a mass of lighter warm air like a huge wedge, making the warm air rise. As this happens, the water vapour in the warm front condenses to form clouds and rain.

A cold front slopes much more steeply than a warm front. Strong updrafts carry moisture up and may bring a short period of heavy rain and storms.

A cold front usually follows a few hours after a warm front. It moves faster than the warm front and will catch it up and merge with it. The warm air is now completely separated, or occluded, from the surface of the Earth.

The front formed when a warm front and a cold front join together is called an occluded front.

BEAUFORT SCALE

The Beaufort scale was invented nearly 200 years ago by Admiral Beaufort. It divides the strength of the wind into a scale from 0 for calm to 12 for hurricane-force winds. For each number, the scale describes the effect of the wind on things around it, such as trees or ocean waves.

Wind power was vital in the days when ships relied on the wind to push them around the globe. The Beaufort scale originally only described the effect of the wind on sailing ships and waves.

0	Calm	Smoke rises up
1	Light air	Smoke drifts
2	Light breeze	Wind felt on face
3	Gentle breeze	Leaves and twigs move
4	Moderate wind	Flags flap
5	Fresh wind	Small trees sway
6	Strong wind	Large branches move
7	Near gale	Whole trees sway
8	Fresh gale	Twigs break off trees
9	Strong gale	Branches break off trees
10	Storm	Trees uprooted
11	Violent storm	Widespread damage
12	Hurricane	Disaster

Rain, hail and snow

The amount of water on the Earth stays the same because it is being constantly recycled by means of the water cycle (*see page 11*). This movement of water between the surface of the Earth and the atmosphere is vital to the existence of all life on Earth. All living things need water to survive.

The air is always moist because it contains invisible water vapour. If the air cools enough, the water vapour condenses into drops of liquid water or ice crystals, which may form clouds, fog, rain or snow. Rain or snow never fall out of a clear, blue sky. They will only fall where there are rising air and clouds.

Clouds form at all levels in the troposphere (*see page 15*), but certain types of cloud are characteristic of different heights above the ground. The shapes, colours and heights of clouds help people to forecast changes in the weather.

snowflake   hailstone

▲ When water vapour in clouds makes ice crystals instead of water droplets, they stick together to form snowflakes, which fall out of the cloud when they are heavy enough. Hailstones grow from ice crystals swept up and down inside a storm cloud. Water freezes around the crystals in layers.

▶ Water evaporates from the oceans and the land, condenses in the sky to form clouds and falls back to Earth as rain or snow. Because of air currents and weather patterns, water evaporating in one place falls as rain far away.

water vapour condenses to form clouds

direction of wind

evaporation from lakes and rivers

evaporation from the soil

evaporation from plants and animals

evaporation from the sea

ground water

Clouds and rain

A cloud is a mass of tiny water droplets suspended in the air. A cloud forms when water vapour condenses on to tiny particles of dust and salt in the air. Layer clouds, such as stratus, form when a spreading mass of warm air rises slowly over a mass of colder air, or over a mountain. Heap clouds, such as cumulus, form when bubbles of warm air rise fast.

For rain to fall, moist air has to rise up into the sky and cool enough for water vapour to condense into liquid water. Air may rise when it is heated by the land or the ocean, when wind blows air up over mountains or hills, or when warm and cold air masses (*see page 40*) meet along a weather front.

Each raindrop is made up of about a million cloud droplets. Rain forms when lots of droplets bump into each other, forming large drops that are too heavy to stay in the sky. They fall out of the cloud as rain. When snowflakes or hailstones fall in warm air, they melt into rain. But when there is cold air all the way to the ground, the snowflakes or hailstones may not melt, but fall to the ground as snow or hail.

Fog is really a cloud nearer the ground. It forms when air near the ground cools and the water vapour condenses into very tiny drops of liquid water which hang in the air. In a fog you may only be able to see 3 metres in front of you.

water falls from clouds as rain, hail, or snow

water drains into streams

the landscape in the rain shadow is dry (see page 35)

water seeps through rocks

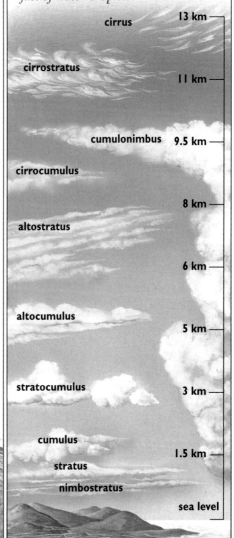

CLOUD TYPES

The main types of cloud (shown below) are in three main families: cirrus (meaning curl of hair), cumulus (meaning heap) and stratus (meaning layer). Clouds are made of ice or water according to their height in the sky. High-level clouds are made of ice crystals. Medium-level clouds are made of water droplets and ice crystals. Low-level clouds are made just of water droplets.

cirrus — 13 km

cirrostratus — 11 km

cumulonimbus — 9.5 km

cirrocumulus

— 8 km

altostratus

— 6 km

altocumulus — 5 km

stratocumulus — 3 km

cumulus

— 1.5 km

stratus

nimbostratus

sea level

Storms

▲**The spiralling clouds of a severe** storm in the Bering Sea, west of Alaska. The photograph was taken by a weather satellite out in space, and false colours have been added by computer to pick out the clouds.

Storms are periods of bad weather, linked to the growth of strong winds and huge clouds in the atmosphere. Winds may blow at over 88.5 kilometres per hour and can even reach over 320 kilometres per hour. Thunderstorms occur where towering cumulonimbus clouds form (*see page 43*) as a result of strong air currents rising along fronts (*see page 41*) or over hot ground. Hurricanes develop from groups of thunderstorms building up over tropical seas. Tornadoes are violent whirlwinds that hang down from thunderclouds. Hurricanes and tornadoes both form in warm, damp air where winds blow into each other from opposite directions. Each has as much energy as several nuclear bombs.

Useful storms

Storms carry heat from the tropics to the poles, helping to even out world temperatures. They stir up the oceans, bringing vital food matter to the surface to feed marine life, and carry water to drought-stricken areas.

Unfortunately, storms can also cause death and destruction, especially since so many people live on or near coasts, where many of the world's most violent storms occur.

Thunder and lightning occur when there is a build-up of different electrical charges inside storm clouds. Strong air currents inside the cloud make ice and water particles bump together, creating static electricity. Negatively charged particles collect at the bottom of the cloud and positively charged ones at the top.

A flash of lighting is a spark of electricity jumping between clouds (sheet lightning) or between the cloud and the ground (fork lightning). It is a way of releasing the energy inside the cloud. Lightning heats up the air and makes it expand at great speed, producing the sonic bang we call thunder.

positive charge

negative charge

◄ A tornado sucks up everything in its path, like a gigantic vacuum cleaner. Tornadoes can pick up people, animals and even small buildings, carrying them over 100 metres before dropping them to the ground. A tornado is like a thin hurricane, with an area of low pressure in the middle.

Hurricanes

Also known as typhoons or cyclones, hurricanes begin life near the equator, where the Sun's heat stirs up moist air over the oceans. Strong winds spiral like a ferris wheel around a calm, central area called the eye. As a hurricane moves, it sucks in warm, moist air near the sea and carries it upward. The warmth feeds the hurricane and makes it stronger. The moisture is then released as torrential rain.

When a hurricane moves over land, its supply of moisture is cut off and it starts to die out. Wind speeds drop, but heavy rain may fall for several days because the air is still rising rapidly. Huge waves as high as 8 metres may flood the coastal areas.

Hurricanes do not move in straight lines, and each one follows a different path. But because they move quite slowly, they can be traced and hurricane warnings given. The energy released in just one hurricane could provide the U.S.A. with electricity for six months.

Tornadoes

The strongest winds of all occur in a tornado. Reliable measurements cannot be made because a tornado will destroy instruments used to measure wind speed, but speeds of perhaps 500 kilometres per hour may occur. A tornado is caused by a strong uplift of air, which sucks in air below, making it spin faster and faster into a funnel shape which extends from a storm cloud to the ground. Tornadoes are most common in the midwest U.S.A., where warm, moist air flows northward from the Gulf of Mexico and cold, dry air from the Rocky Mountains flows on top of it. Strong upward currents of air often develop and may produce a tornado. Tornadoes tend to be narrow funnels, but can also be up to 100 metres across and travel for more than 200 kilometres.

45

▲ **The rocks on this beach** in southern England show the powerful effects of wind and water constantly wearing away the Earth's surface and carving it into new shapes.

LANDSHAPES

AS WIND, WATER AND ICE MOVE OVER THE surface of the Earth, they carve out valleys, cliffs and caves, and build up hills, beaches and sand dunes.

Deserts

Deserts cover about a third of the Earth's land. They are places where more water is lost through evaporation than falls as rain and where there is usually less than 25 centimetres of rain a year. The biggest deserts occur in areas where there are belts of warm, dry, sinking air. Other deserts are in mountain rain shadows (*see page 35*), in the dry centre of continents, or near the poles, where hardly any snow falls.

▲ **The Gobi Desert** in central Asia is a cold desert with hot summers and cold winters. The nomadic people who live here use Bactrian camels for transportation, food, tents and fuel.

mesa: a broad, flat-topped hill with steep sides

wadi: a dried-up watercourse

▲ **Since few plants can** survive in a hot, dry desert landscape, the land is exposed to attack by wind and water, forming striking land shapes. Most deserts are rocky or stony, and only 20 percent have sand dunes.

Water and wind erosion

Heavy rain occasionally falls in a desert and may carve out steep-sided valleys called wadis. These remain dry most of the time. Desert hills called mesas and smaller ones called buttes were probably also shaped by water, but this happened many years ago when the climate was wetter and the area was not a desert. Some deserts still have rivers flowing through them, although the water now comes from rainy areas outside the desert.

These desert rivers flow at the bottom of deep, steep-sided valleys called canyons, such as the Grand Canyon, through which the Colorado River flows.

Desert winds can reach almost 100 kilometres per hour because there is little vegetation to slow them down. The wind flings grains of sand against the rock, wearing it away to form arches, mushroom or pedestal rocks, or rock ridges.

Sand dunes

In flat deserts, tiny bits of rock are blown by the wind into heaps, called sand dunes, which change and move with the wind. A dune's shape depends on the wind speed and direction, how much sand there is and whether there is any plant cover.

butte: a smaller version of a mesa

mushroom rock

pedestal rock

eroded arch

a barchan dune is curved

direction of wind

a seif dune is straight

a star dune forms where the wind blows from all directions

a transverse dune forms at a right angle to the wind

hamada: a bare, rocky pavement

oasis: a patch of vegetation where water is on or near the surface

direction of wind

▲ **Desert sand** is blown along about 45 centimetres above the ground in a series of hops, by a process called saltation. As the grains of sand land, they hit other grains and either bounce off into the air themselves, or push other grains off the ground. The surface of a desert is made up of millions of dancing grains.

Life in deserts

Wildlife in deserts must adapt to an uncertain climate. Rain may not fall for months, or even years. The soil becomes parched until it is dry as dust. Then comes torrential rain.

Living things also have to survive large daily temperature changes – from over 38°C during the day to 10°C at night. In a desert, there are few clouds or plants to hold the heat near the ground at night. Because of the lack of plants, only small numbers of plant-eating animals can survive. There are even fewer hunters, such as foxes and snakes, that feed on plant eaters. So desert wildlife is rare, scattered and very well adapted. People who live in deserts face similar problems.

addax
fennec fox
gerbil
jerboa

Wildlife

Most desert animals survive with very little water. Some, such as the kangaroo rat and the addax, do not drink at all, but get all the moisture they need from their food. Animals such as the camel and the Gila monster store fat in their bodies to keep them going when food and water are scarce.

Smaller animals hide away in burrows during the day and come out at night, when it is cooler and damper. The large ears of the kit fox and the jackrabbit act like radiators to give off heat.

Animals that come out during the day must move across hot, soft sand. The camel and the addax

Costa's hummingbird
red-tailed hawk
elf owl
saguaro cactus
jackrabbit
Gila monster
kit fox
rattlesnake
kangaroo rat
scorpion

◀ **The North American deserts** cover large areas of the southwestern United States and northern Mexico. The Sonoran Desert in Mexico is famous for the giant saguaro cactus. It may grow up to 15 metres tall and live for over 200 years.

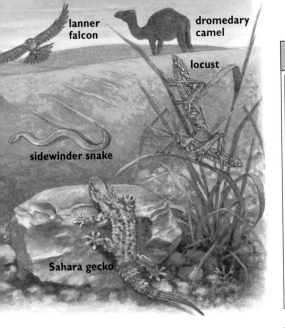

- lanner falcon
- dromedary camel
- locust
- sidewinder snake
- Sahara gecko

WATER IN THE DESERT

In some desert places, water comes to the surface to form a moist area called an oasis, where plants can grow. The water often comes from rain that has fallen on mountains hundreds of kilometres away and drained through underground rocks. The water and plants in an oasis are vital for desert people and animals. People may settle near an oasis and use the water to grow crops.

- rain falls on mountains
- water seeps through underground rocks
- oasis
- water on the surface
- fault

▲ **The Sahara** is the largest, hottest desert in the world. It stretches across most of northern Africa. Saharan animals include the dromedary camel, which can go without water for several weeks.

have wide feet to stop them from sinking. The hairy paws of the sand cat do the same job, and keep the heat out as well. The sidewinder snake loops sideways across the sand, hardly touching the surface.

Some lizards stand on three or two legs at a time to let their limbs cool.

The lack of water is also a problem for desert plants. Some, such as mesquite trees, have long roots to tap water deep underground. Others, such as cacti, have roots that spread out near the surface to catch as much moisture as possible. Many desert plants, including cacti, are succulents. They store water in swollen stems, leaves or underground roots to last them through periods of drought.

Some plants spend most of their lives as seeds, lying in the desert soil waiting for heavy rainfall. Then they sprout, flower, produce seeds and die, all in the few weeks it takes for the ground to dry out again.

The balance of life in deserts is fragile and easily destroyed by people. New boreholes mean people pump much more water from the ground and can keep more animals, which may overgraze the land. Once the plant cover is removed, the dry soil is easily blown or washed away. People dig up desert plants to sell, and many desert animals have been hunted almost to extinction.

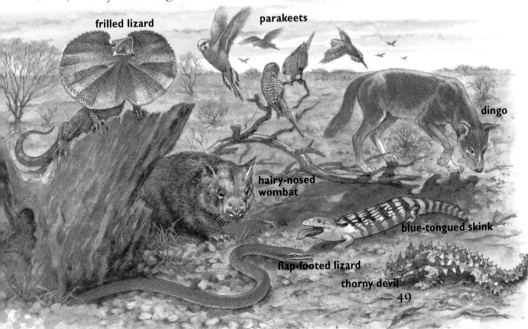

- frilled lizard
- parakeets
- dingo
- hairy-nosed wombat
- blue-tongued skink
- flap-footed lizard
- thorny devil

◄ **Dry, desertlike land** covers more than two-thirds of Australia. It is rich in lizards – such as the frilled lizard and the thorny devil – which can survive higher temperatures than birds or mammals.

49

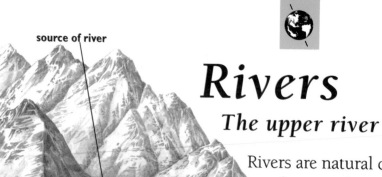

source of river

V-shaped valley

Rivers
The upper river

Rivers are natural channels that carry water downhill because of the pull of gravity (*see page 9*). They may snake across the surface, or under the ground, wearing away the land and depositing the material they are carrying (*see page 10*). The way a river flows depends on the rocks, soil, climate and how people use it. Most major cities grew up near rivers because they can be used for many things including drinking water, farming, industry, energy and recreation.

tributary

Sources of rivers
The start of a river is often just a natural hollow in the ground where water seeps in from the surrounding soil to start a flow of water. Even huge rivers such as the Amazon in South America or the Nile in Africa start like this. Some rivers are fed by underground springs, especially in limestone areas where water drains easily through the rocks. Other rivers may flow from a marsh, a lake or the end of a glacier.

Drainage patterns
From a trickle of water at its source, a river grows steadily larger as small streams, called tributaries, add water to the main channel.

The shape made by a river and its tributaries is called a drainage pattern. The shape of this pattern depends on the type of soil and rock, how steeply the land slopes and earth movements under the ground. Rivers often form a branching

▲ **The upper river** usually carves out a narrow, V-shaped valley and cuts down into the land, winding around obstacles, to form tongues of land called spurs which jut out from the valley sides. The speed of the water is slowed down by all the stones, pebbles and grit bouncing along the river bed.

drainage pattern, known as dendritic drainage. If a river and its tributaries flow outward from a central high point, this is called a radial drainage pattern.

▲ **This satellite picture shows the** branching, dendritic drainage pattern of the De Grey River, which flows across the Norton Plain in Western Australia. The green patches show rocks that were formed in the days of the dinosaurs.

DAMMING RIVERS

A dam is built across a river to hold back the water, which forms a lake called a reservoir behind the dam. The water in the reservoir may be used for drinking, fishing, recreation or to irrigate farmland. In some dams, such as the Hoover Dam on the Colorado River, in the United States (right), electricity is generated from water falling inside the dam. Electricity generated this way is called hydroelectric power.

Dams can cause problems. For example, there is less water downstream for farmers and wildlife, and reservoir water may be lost through evaporation.

Shaping the land
A river wears away the land mainly by scratching and scraping the rocks and soil with its load – the material it carries. This process is called abrasion. A river's load breaks up into smaller pieces as rocks and pebbles bump into each other. This is called attrition.

A river moves its load in three main ways, depending on the size of the particles. Very small particles are dissolved in the water. Larger particles of sand or grit hang or float in the water. The biggest pieces of stone and gravel move by rolling, tumbling or bouncing along the river bed.

▶ **Potholes mark the places** where the river water swirls pebbles round and round. This wears away the river bed to form a deep, pot-shaped hole.

▼ **A river may form a network** of channels around islands of gravel and sand. This is called braiding. It happens if the river is too shallow to sweep a lot of coarse sediment along.

waterfall

▲ **A waterfall** happens where a river comes to a band of hard rock with soft rock on the other side. The soft rock wears away, leaving a ledge over which the river flows as a waterfall. A plunge pool may form at the bottom of the waterfall where soft rock is carved out by boulders whirling around.

braiding

Rivers
The lower river

As a river gets farther from its source, it carries more water and sediment. The land becomes flatter and the river cuts sideways into it, creating a wider, flatter valley. The river begins to swing more from side to side in curves called meanders. It also drops some of the sediment it is carrying. When the river ends its journey, in the sea or in a lake, it drops the rest of the sediment to form a delta. Along the course of this tropical river in South America, you can see some of the plants and animals that are adapted to living in this habitat.

▲ **The Grand Canyon** in North America took millions of years to form. Layers of sediment, deposited by seas and rivers, gradually built up and were compressed into sandstone rock. Later, the Colorado River cut into the rock and the Grand Canyon was formed.

▼ **Giant water lilies** can be nearly 1 metre across and strong enough to hold a child. Underneath they have thorns to protect them from plant-eating fish.

▲ **A baby hoatzin** uses claws on its wings to climb trees along the river bank. It leaps into the water to avoid danger.

▼ **Electric eels** often live in holes beneath a river bank. Electric eels use pulses of electricity for finding their way in muddy waters, as well as for catching their prey. They can kill by electrocution.

oxbow lake (see page 58)

▲ **Capybaras** live in family groups by the water's edge. They have webbed toes and are excellent swimmers. Capybaras are the world's largest rodents.

Floodplains

When a river floods, it covers the floodplain – the flat land on either side – with water containing bits of sand and mud. The heaviest sediment (sand and gravel) is dropped first, near the river, forming low walls called levees. The water carries the lighter sediment (fine clays and silt) farther away from the river. When the floodwaters go down, a thin sheet of mud and silt is left behind on the floodplain.

After many floods, this builds up into layers of fertile mud called alluvium, which is good for farming.

Delta shapes

As a river enters a lake or the sea, it slows down. It drops its load of sediment, which may form a fan shape, called a delta. A delta grows where a river drops sediment faster than tides or currents can carry it away. Heavier particles of sand and gravel drop to the bottom, while lighter particles are carried farther away. The sediment builds up in layers, like a sandwich.

The shape of a coastal delta depends on how much water and sediment the river carries and the strength and speed of waves, currents and tides. Strong waves may force the sediment to spread out to make a pointed shape with curved sides. Calm water may let a delta build up "toes" of sediment into the sea. The delta of the Mississippi River in the United States form a bird's-foot shape like the one below.

FLOOD CONTROL

To prevent rivers from flooding, people build barriers, or embankments called levees, made of sand, rock and cement. A barrier or levee may help to control floods in one areas, but water is forced up or downstream, increasing problems in other areas. Barriers may also affect river wildlife because the variety of habitats is reduced.

◄ **Anacondas** attack animals that come to the river to drink, squeezing the life out of them before swallowing them whole.

◄ **River dolphins** rely on a system called echolocation to find food in murky river waters. They send out high-pitched clicking sounds and time how long the clicks take to bounce off things around them.

► **A crocodile** uses its strong tail to push itself through the water. Its snout is lined with many pointed teeth to spear fish.

▼ **A typical river delta** has a triangular shape. The name comes from the Greek letter delta, which is shaped like a triangle. On the surface of a delta, a river splits into a branching network of channels. These channels are called distributaries.

deposited sediment

delta

sea

meander

▲ **Meanders are curves** which occur as the water twists and turns naturally over the land. The river cuts cliffs into the outside bends of meanders, and material is deposited on inside bends to form small beaches.

◄ **Most piranhas** live mainly on fruit and nuts. When plant food is hard to find, some may eat meat. Piranhas detect food from vibrations in the water, which they pick up using a sense organ, called a lateral line, along the side of their body.

Caves

Underground caves are some of the last unexplored parts of the Earth's crust. Many caves are huge, stretching deep under the ground for up to 1,200 metres, and may include chambers big enough to hold several football pitches.

Caves are often formed by water eating away rock to form tunnels and "rooms" in limestone rock. Pieces of rock left behind often form amazing patterns of spikes, steps and columns. Caves can also form inside coastal cliffs or inside glaciers. A network of caves may be left underneath a lava flow (*see page 26*) when the liquid lava has drained away, leaving empty tunnels behind. Most caves are dark, cold, wet places where few animals and plants survive.

▲ **An ice cave** may form inside an iceberg (*above*). Ice caves also form inside glaciers where the ice pulls apart as it goes around a bend, or a river flowing under a glacier melts the ice. The rising heat of a geothermal spring may melt a glacier from the inside to form a cave.

A **sinkhole** forms where a joint in the rock is eaten away by rainwater, leaving a deep vertical shaft. Water may flow down the hole to form an underground waterfall.

Water sinks down to the water table – the layer where the rock is already full of water and can hold no more. Then the water runs along the top of this wet rock to form an underground river.

Dripping water evaporates, leaving the dissolved rock as a mineral called calcite. Calcite "icicles" called stalactites hang down from cave roofs. Spikes of calcite jutting up from the cave floor are called stalagmites.

CAVE ANIMALS

Since plants need light to make food, they cannot survive in dark caves. Cave animals are adapted to living without light or plants to eat. The main source of food is the droppings of creatures such as bats and birds which roost in caves, seeking shelter from predators and the weather.

A pile of bat droppings may be teeming with millipedes and insects such as springtails, beetles, cockroaches and cave crickets. Because caves are dark, many cave animals are blind and rely instead on their senses of touch and smell to guide them.

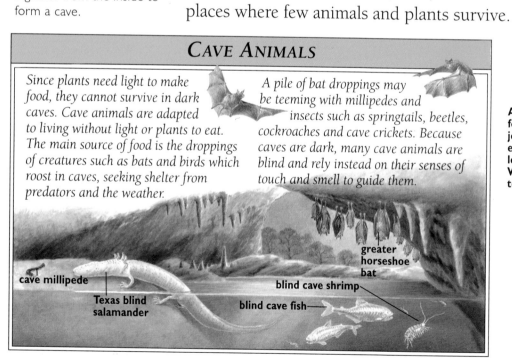

cave millipede

Texas blind salamander

greater horseshoe bat

blind cave shrimp

blind cave fish

Limestone caves

Rainwater erodes limestone easily because it contains acids that dissolve calcium carbonate, the main ingredient of limestone. Rainwater can dissolve a few millimetres of limestone in a year, so it takes a long time to form a large cave system.

As the rainwater seeps into vertical and horizontal cracks in the limestone rock, it makes the cracks wider and wider until a large space called a cave forms. The biggest caves are called caverns.

Sea and lava caves

The pounding of the sea breaks up coastal rocks along its lines of weakness. The power of the water also squashes air into cracks in the rocks, and this pushes against the rocks, helping to split them apart to form caves.

Lava caves may form where the surface of the lava cools down, making a solid roof. This stops the lava underneath from cooling down, so it keeps flowing. When the hot lava drains away, it leaves behind long tunnels, which form caves.

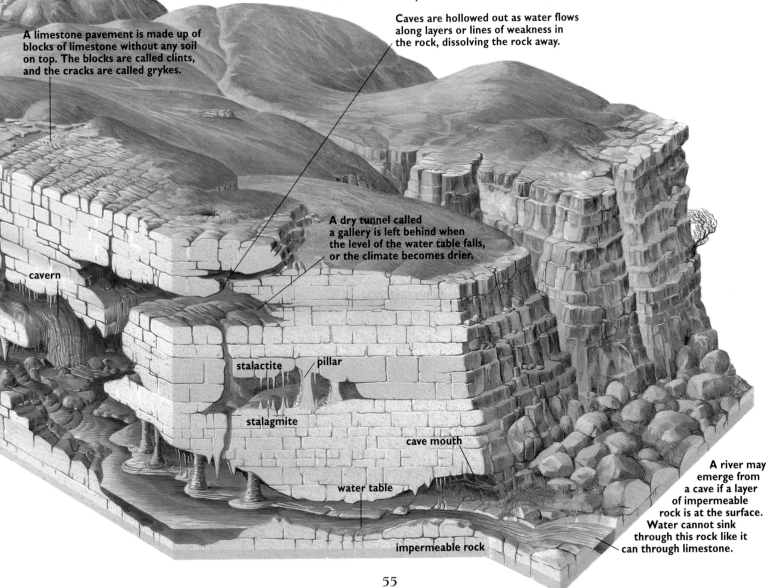

A limestone pavement is made up of blocks of limestone without any soil on top. The blocks are called clints, and the cracks are called grykes.

Caves are hollowed out as water flows along layers or lines of weakness in the rock, dissolving the rock away.

A dry tunnel called a gallery is left behind when the level of the water table falls, or the climate becomes drier.

cavern

stalactite   pillar

stalagmite

cave mouth

water table

impermeable rock

A river may emerge from a cave if a layer of impermeable rock is at the surface. Water cannot sink through this rock like it can through limestone.

Glaciers

Ice covers about 10 percent of the Earth's land and 12 percent of the oceans. Large areas of ice form at the poles and on high mountains, where more snow falls in winter than melts in summer. Layers of ice, called ice sheets, cover huge areas – an ice sheet one and a half times the size of the U.S.A. covers Antarctica. Glaciers are "rivers" of ice that usually form in mountain valleys. The ice in glaciers and ice sheets is pulled slowly downhill by gravity. The ice drags rocks and pebbles along with it, which act like sandpaper, eroding the land into new shapes (*see page 10*). When the ice melts, the material it was carrying is left behind, forming hills, ridges and gravel-covered plains.

▲ **In polar regions** glaciers and ice sheets extend into the sea. Huge chunks of ice snap off and float away as icebergs. Some are so huge they can be tracked by satellites. Arctic icebergs are usually tall, with an uneven shape. Antarctic icebergs (*above*) have a flatter shape.

How glaciers move

In most glaciers there are two sorts of movement. Sometimes the pressure of the weight of ice melts the bottom of the glacier, and the ice slips over the rocks on this thin layer of melted ice. Or, layers of ice in a glacier may slide over each other when the surface flows faster than the base, pulling this ice along.

Although glaciers move slowly – several centimetres to less than a metre a day – their huge size and weight gives them great power to wear away the land. As water from ice melting on the surface of the glacier works its way into the rock under the glacier and refreezes, pieces of rock break loose and freeze

lateral moraine

medial moraine

kettle hole

esker

drumlins

snout, or end, of glacier

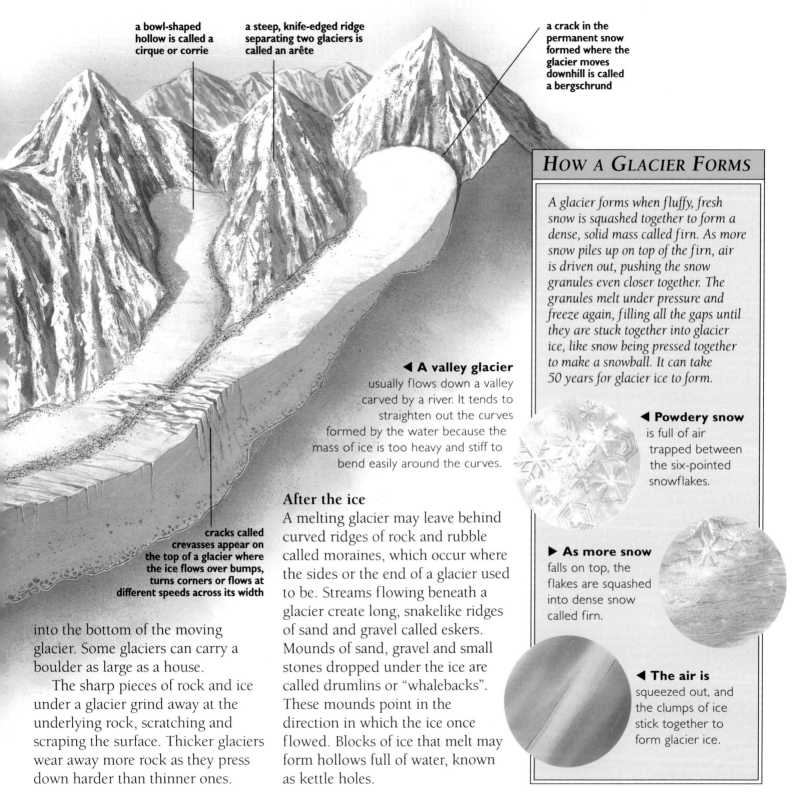

a bowl-shaped hollow is called a cirque or corrie

a steep, knife-edged ridge separating two glaciers is called an arête

a crack in the permanent snow formed where the glacier moves downhill is called a bergschrund

HOW A GLACIER FORMS

A glacier forms when fluffy, fresh snow is squashed together to form a dense, solid mass called firn. As more snow piles up on top of the firn, air is driven out, pushing the snow granules even closer together. The granules melt under pressure and freeze again, filling all the gaps until they are stuck together into glacier ice, like snow being pressed together to make a snowball. It can take 50 years for glacier ice to form.

◀ **A valley glacier** usually flows down a valley carved by a river. It tends to straighten out the curves formed by the water because the mass of ice is too heavy and stiff to bend easily around the curves.

◀ **Powdery snow** is full of air trapped between the six-pointed snowflakes.

After the ice

A melting glacier may leave behind curved ridges of rock and rubble called moraines, which occur where the sides or the end of a glacier used to be. Streams flowing beneath a glacier create long, snakelike ridges of sand and gravel called eskers. Mounds of sand, gravel and small stones dropped under the ice are called drumlins or "whalebacks". These mounds point in the direction in which the ice once flowed. Blocks of ice that melt may form hollows full of water, known as kettle holes.

▶ **As more snow** falls on top, the flakes are squashed into dense snow called firn.

cracks called crevasses appear on the top of a glacier where the ice flows over bumps, turns corners or flows at different speeds across its width

◀ **The air is** squeezed out, and the clumps of ice stick together to form glacier ice.

into the bottom of the moving glacier. Some glaciers can carry a boulder as large as a house.

The sharp pieces of rock and ice under a glacier grind away at the underlying rock, scratching and scraping the surface. Thicker glaciers wear away more rock as they press down harder than thinner ones.

Lakes

A lake is a hollow or valley filled with still water. The water can be either fresh or salty. The hollows in which lakes form may be created by glaciers or ice sheets (*see page 56*) carving dips in the land, or by movements inside the Earth making cracks in the crust. Sometimes lakes form where the path of a river is blocked by a landslide, by rocks and mud left behind by glaciers, or by dams built by people or beavers. Lakes are an important refuge for wildlife, especially birds, fish and insects, and people use lakes for fishing, transportation, water supplies and recreation.

▲ An oxbow lake forms where a river cuts through a U-shaped bend, or meander (*see page 53*), leaving a curved lake behind. In time, an oxbow lake may fill in with mud and plants.

▶ A crater lake forms where water fills a hollow at the top of an extinct volcano. A caldera (*see page 27*) can also fill with rain to become a lake, such as Crater Lake, Oregon, U.S.A.

▼ Forces inside the Earth may create a dip on the surface that fills with water to form a lake. The deep lakes in the African Rift Valley, such as Lake Tanganyika, were formed by faulting.

▲ This hotel in Bolivia has been built on a salt lake and is made of blocks of salt. The surface of the lake consists of the salty deposits left behind when water in the lake evaporated into the air.

Glacial lakes

Many lakes are the result of erosion by the glaciers and ice sheets that covered the land during the last Ice Age, about 18,000 years ago. The ice scoured out troughs in the surface of the land as it moved over it. When the climate warmed up and the ice melted, water filled these hollows to form lakes. Melted glaciers and ice sheets also left behind large deposits of soil and pebbles. This material sometimes formed dams that trapped water, allowing more lakes to form. Lake Como in Italy was formed like this. In North America, the weight of a huge ice sheet made the land sink into a basin. After the ice melted, water filled up the basin to form the Great Lakes.

Earth movements

The world's deepest lakes were formed by movements within the Earth making its crust crumple up or break apart. Water filled up cracks in the crust to make deep lakes such as Lake Tanganyika in East Africa and Lake Baikal in Siberia – at up to 1,637 metres deep, the deepest lake in the world.

The Caspian Sea, between southeastern Europe and Asia, was formed when a new block of land was pushed up and cut off a piece of ocean to make a lake. The Caspian Sea is the world's largest lake, with an area of about 371,000 square kilometres.

▼ Lakes eventually disappear as they are filled in with mud, silt and plants, or are drained by rivers. Lakes may also dry up if the climate gets hotter and they lose more water through evaporation than they gain from rivers. Disappearing lakes produce many of the world's marshes, swamps and bogs.

Saltwater lakes

These lakes usually form in a hot climate where the exits from them become cut off by folds or faults in the Earth's crust (*see pages 32–33*). Water escapes mainly by evaporation (*see page 11*), leaving salt behind. A lake that starts out with fresh water may gradually become saltier.

The Dead Sea, between Israel and Jordan, is 8 times saltier than seawater. About 10 centimetres of rain fall each year, but nearly 2 metres of water is lost through evaporation. Lake Natron in the African Rift Valley (*see page 22*) is salty not just because of evaporation, but because the lake is fed by volcanic springs which bring salty minerals into the lake.

▲ At the start of a glacier, a cirque (*see page 57*) may fill with water when the ice melts. This forms circular lakes, such as the ones called tarns, found in the English Lake District.

◀ An erosion lake forms when water collects in hollows gouged from the rock by passing ice sheets.

Waves, tides and coasts

The power of the waves, currents and tides constantly changes the shape of the coastline. Waves are driven by the wind, while tides are caused by the pull of gravity from both the Moon and the Sun. In some places the coast is eroded away to form features such as cliffs, bays, stacks or arches. In other places sand, pebbles and shells build up to form beaches, spits and marshes. Sometimes the wind blows the sand on beaches into little hills called dunes.

For the last 15,000 years, as the climate has become warmer, the sea level has been rising and "drowning" the coasts. A drowned coast may be marked by an estuary – a river mouth drowned by the tide – or by a fjord, a valley cut by a glacier which is now flooded by the sea. Salt marshes form in estuaries as plants trap mud in their roots and gradually increase the marsh's level.

▲ **Mangrove trees grow** in coastal or river swamps in tropical countries. Swamp mud contains little oxygen, so the mangrove roots stick up above the mud to absorb the oxygen they need.

estuary

sand spit

salt marsh

sand dunes

groynes are low barriers built to stop longshore drift

a lagoon is a lake cut off from the sea

bars are low ridges of sand and pebbles that pile up offshore parallel to the coast

Wave erosion

Waves hurl pebbles and rocks against the shore, which increases their cutting power. Air is squashed into cracks in the rocks, and when the wave pulls back, the air explodes, bursting the rocks apart. The chemicals in sea water also help to dissolve soft rocks such as chalk and limescale.

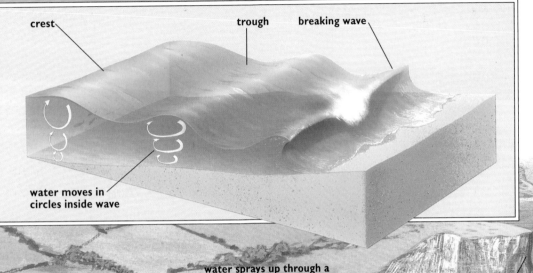

The wind whips up the surface of the sea into waves. A wave's height, length and speed is controlled by the wind speed, the length of time that the wind blows and the distance that the wind blows over the water.

The water within each wave stays in almost the same place, moving in circles. Near the shore, some of this water catches against the seabed. This slows the wave down, so the top curves over and breaks.

crest

trough

breaking wave

water moves in circles inside wave

water sprays up through a blow hole in the cave roof

headland

sea cave

stack

bay

arch

Soft rock wears away faster than hard rock to form bays, with hard rock forming headlands. As these are worn away and material is deposited in bays, the coastline is smoothed out. Wave erosion of headlands also creates cliffs, which may have sea caves, cut by waves in weak rock. If waves cut away caves on both sides of a headland, a rock arch forms. If the top of the arch collapses, a tall pillar of rock called a stack is left just off the coast.

Beaches

Loose pebbles and sand form as waves erode the coast or when rivers deposit material as they flow into the sea. Some of this material is transported along the coast by the waves and builds up into a beach. Beach material is often pulled along sideways by the waves. This is called longshore drift. If there is a break in the coastline, longshore drift may push the beach material out into the sea to form a long, thin ridge called a spit. The waves may push the end of the spit into a curved shape.

Tides

The sea level rises and falls daily as the Moon's gravity (*see page 9*) pulls the water in the Earth's oceans. The Sun's gravity also pulls the oceans, but its effect is weaker because the Sun is much farther from Earth.

As the Moon and the Earth orbit the Sun, their positions change. When the three are in a line, the pull of the Sun and Moon give extra high tides and extra low tides, called spring tides. When the Sun, the Moon and the Earth form a right angle, high tides are at their lowest and low tides are at their highest. These are called neap tides. Each month there are two spring tides and two neap tides.

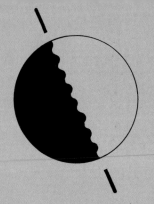

THE WHOLE EARTH

MAPS HELP US TO RECORD INFORMATION ABOUT THE EARTH. More accurate mapping in the future, including the use of satellite images, will help us understand how the Earth works, so that we are able to take better care of the planet.

Mapping the world

A globe is the only truly accurate map of the world, but globes are expensive to make and difficult to carry around. A flat map is easy to fold up and carry and can show details of small areas of the Earth. The different ways of drawing the Earth's curved surface on to a piece of paper are called map projections. All projections distort area, shape, distance or direction in some way.

▲ Most maps today are drawn with north at the top and south at the bottom. A compass is used to point a map in the right direction by lining up the magnetic needle on the compass with north on the map.

▲ This satellite photo of the Earth looking down over the North Pole gives an unfamiliar view of our planet. It shows how the North Pole is surrounded by land masses.

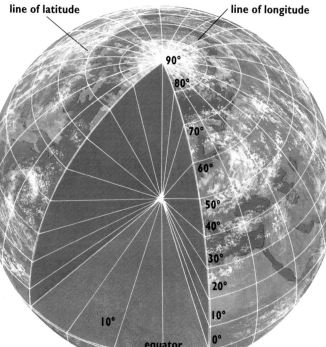

line of latitude   line of longitude

90°
80°
70°
60°
50°
40°
30°
20°
10°
10°
0°
equator

Latitude and longitude

Lines of latitude and longitude are imaginary lines drawn around the globe to make it easier for people to draw maps and pinpoint places. Lines of latitude are circles around the world parallel to the equator. They are sometimes called parallels. Lines of longitude are lines drawn up and down the world from pole to pole. They are also known as meridians.

◄ Lines of latitude and longitude are measured in degrees, which represent the angles between the lines and the centre of the Earth.

Distances in degrees

The lines of latitude are distances in degrees north or south of the equator. Places on the equator have a latitude of 0° (degrees), the North Pole has a latitude of 90° North and the South Pole has a latitude of 90° South. The lines of latitude are 111 kilometres apart.

Lines of longitude are the distance in degrees east or west of an imaginary line running from the North Pole to the South Pole. This line, called the prime meridian, has a longitude of 0°. It passes through the district of Greenwich in London, England. There are 180 degrees east and 180 degrees west of the prime meridian. These lines of longitude meet at the poles and they are widest apart at the equator.

Every place on Earth can be found from a longitude and latitude reference. For example, New York City is 40° north and 73° west, while London is 53° north and 0° west or east.

Map projections

All map projections involve stretching or shrinking parts of the globe. Some give the sizes of the land accurately, but the shapes of the land masses are wrong. Others give the shapes of the land accurately, but their relative sizes are wrong.

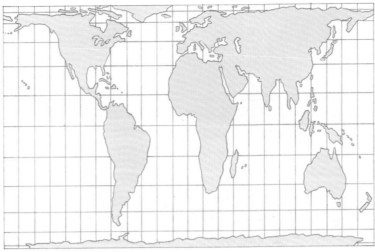

◀ Peters' projection gives the countries of the southern hemisphere their true importance by showing the sizes of the land areas accurately, but the land shapes are distorted.

▶ A cylindrical projection, such as Mercator's, is made as if a light is shining through a globe on to a cylinder wrapped around it. The poles do not appear on this projection, and it makes the countries near the poles appear too large.

◀ A conical projection is made as if a light shines through a globe on to a cone of paper wrapped around it. The cone is then spread out into a flat fan shape. The most accurate part of the map is where the cone touches the globe. Conical projections show areas, distances and directions fairly accurately.

▶ Planar projections are made as if one point on the globe was touching a piece of paper. This sort of projection is circular, but can show only half the world at a time. It shows true directions from one point to another, but the shapes are distorted farther away from the centre.

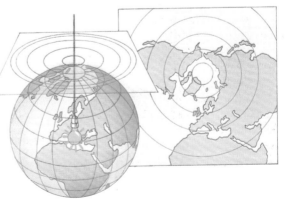

Future of the Earth

Ever since the Earth formed about 4.6 billion years ago, it has been constantly changing. The continents have moved, the surface of the planet has been shaped by wind, rain and ice, and living creatures, including the dinosaurs, have come and gone. The gases in the Earth's atmosphere have also changed over the years, and the climate has become warmer and cooler at different times. Nowadays, pollution is creating new problems, such as acid rain, global warming and holes in the ozone layer.

▶ **The Sun's ultraviolet rays** pass through holes in the ozone layer. The holes are caused mainly by gases in refrigerators, air conditioning, some spray cans, some plastic packaging and insulation materials.

▼ **When gases from vehicle exhausts** and power plants mix with water in the air, rain becomes much more acidic. "Acid rain" weakens trees and damages their growth, especially trees with needlelike leaves, such as pine trees.

Ice ages

At times, the Earth's climate has been much colder than it is now. These "ice ages" may have been caused by a decrease in the Sun's heat, or a change in the angle of the Earth's tilt on its axis, or a change in its path around the Sun. We are now living in a warm period, but there may be another ice age in the future.

Global warming

Many scientists believe that world temperatures are rising due to a build-up of certain gases in the atmosphere. Gases, such as carbon dioxide, water vapour, methane and nitrogen oxides, are given off by power plants, factories, vehicles, farm animals, farm fields, rotting garbage and the burning of forest trees. The gases trap heat given off by the Earth and stop it from getting too cold, but too many of these gases may overheat the world. This may cause ice to melt and the oceans to rise, flooding coastal areas. Droughts and food shortages may also occur in the tropics.

Better energy conservation, reduction in pollution from power plants and factories, and greater use of renewable energy such as wind, water and wave power, would all reduce future global warming.

hole in ozone layer

ozone layer stops most ultraviolet rays from reaching ground

harmful ultraviolet rays reach ground

Ozone holes

Ozone (*see page 15*) keeps out harmful ultraviolet rays from the Sun. In larger doses, these rays can cause skin cancers and eye problems. Plants and animals are also damaged by too much ultraviolet light. In the Antarctic, high levels of ultraviolet radiation stop tiny plants called plankton– the basis of food chains in the ocean – from making food.

Large holes in the ozone layer have been found over the Antarctic, the Arctic, Australia and New Zealand, as well as a general thinning of ozone all over the planet. The main reason for ozone holes seems to be chemicals such as CFCs, which attack and break down the ozone layer. Another cause is the huge amounts of dust and ash thrown into the atmosphere by volcanic eruptions (*see page 26*).

BIOSPHERE PROJECT

In the Biosphere project in the Arizona desert, scientists created climate zones (see page 37) on a tiny scale in sealed glasshouses. About 3,800 species of plants and animals lived with eight scientists inside the biosphere for two years. The scientists lived without outside help, grew their own food and recycled their wastes. They found out about how the Earth's living systems work and planned how the first settlers in space could survive far away from Earth.

▼ **A build-up of certain gases** in the atmosphere is believed to be causing global warming – the heating up of the whole Earth. The gases keep heat given off by Earth from escaping into space.

heat escapes into space

Earth's heat cannot escape into space

solar roof generates electricity

bedrooms and living rooms face south to catch the Sun

walls and roof, floors and windows are well insulated to stop heat loss

triple-glazed windows

rain water collected from roof and drained to basement tanks

waste recycled

electric car

▲ **The Oxford Eco House, England,** shows one way that people could live in the future, by causing less pollution and using fewer of the Earth's resources. The house was designed to use as little energy as possible for heating, cooling and lighting. A solar roof converts the Sun's energy into electricity for use in the house and to power an electric car.

Glossary

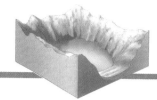

Most words dealing with the Earth are explained in the text. So try looking in the index if you cannot find the word you are looking for here.

acid rain Rain that is more acidic than usual due to all the chemicals from power plants and vehicle exhausts mixed in with it.

anticyclone A large area of high pressure (also called a high) from which all winds blow outward. Anticyclones give settled weather.

atmosphere The blanket of gases around a planet, held there by the pull of the planet's gravity. The Earth's atmosphere is about 800 kilometres high.

billion One thousand million.

caldera A shallow depression at the top of a volcano formed by an eruption, or by the collapse of a volcanic cone into the vent.

climate The average weather in a place over a long period of time.

condensation The process by which a gas or a vapour changes into a liquid as it cools.

continental drift The way the continents slowly drift about the globe because of forces deep inside the Earth.

core The metallic centre of the Earth, made of a molten (liquid) outer core and a solid inner core.

Coriolis effect The way that winds and water are twisted by the spin of the Earth – to the right in the northern hemisphere and to the left in the southern hemisphere.

crust The rocky "skin" that forms a thin shell over the Earth's surface. There are two main types of crust: oceanic and continental.

delta A build-up of sand and silt where a river slows down and drops its load as it enters a lake or the ocean.

depression An area of low pressure which brings unsettled weather. It may also be called a low or a cyclone.

dissolve To make a solid substance or a gas disappear into a liquid.

energy The power to do work and make things happen. There are different forms of energy, such as light, sound, heat and movement.

epicentre The point on the Earth's surface directly above an earthquake's focus, which is the place below the ground where the earthquake starts.

erosion The removal of material on the Earth's surface by wind, running water, or ice in glaciers and ice sheets.

equator An imaginary line which divides the Earth into two halves, halfway between the North and South poles.

evaporation The process by which a liquid is changed into a vapour or a gas when it is heated.

fault A crack in the Earth's crust where blocks of rock slip past each other.

floodplain A flat area of land on both sides of a river channel near the end of its course.

A floodplain is formed from layers of sediment deposited when the river overflows its banks.

fold A bend in the layers of rock which make up the Earth's crust.

fossil The remains or shape of an animal or plant preserved in rock.

front The boundary between two masses of air of different temperatures. Rain often occurs along a front.

galaxy A vast cluster of stars, gas and dust out in space held together by gravity. The Earth is in a galaxy called the Milky Way.

geothermal energy Energy that comes from heat deep inside the Earth.

geyser A natural hot spring that shoots up hot water and steam at intervals through a hole in the Earth's crust.

global warming The warming of the Earth's atmosphere due to pollution.

gravity An invisible force that pulls every object in the Universe toward every other object. The pull of gravity depends on how heavy an object is. The strongest pull comes from gigantic objects such as planets and stars. Gravity gives things weight.

hemisphere One half of a sphere. The Earth is divided by the equator into the northern hemisphere and the southern hemisphere.

hydroelectric power Electricity generated by using the force of moving water. "Hydro" means water.

igneous rock A rock formed by the cooling and hardening of hot liquid magma or lava.

impermeable rock Rock which does not allow water to pass through it easily.

jet stream   Very fast wind circling the globe high in the atmosphere – between 10 and 16 kilometres above the Earth's surface.

lava   The name given to molten rock (magma) from inside the Earth when it reaches the surface.

lines of latitude   Imaginary lines that run horizontally around the Earth and measure the distance from the equator. The equator is at 0° and the poles are at 90° of latitude.

lines of longitude   Imaginary lines that run at right angles to the equator and meet at the North and South poles.

longshore drift   The movement of sediment parallel to the shore when waves strike the shore at an angle.

magma   Hot, liquid (molten) rock in the Earth's mantle and crust deep underground. Magma sometimes comes out on to the surface through volcanoes.

mantle   The rocky middle layer of the Earth, between the outer crust and the inner core.

map projection   A way of drawing the curved surface of the Earth on to a flat map. There are hundreds of different map projections.

metamorphic rock   A rock formed when igneous or sedimentary rocks are altered by heat and pressure.

meander   A curve in the course of a river.

mineral   A natural substance in the Earth's crust which has a definite chemical composition and does not come from animals or plants.

monsoon   A wind which blows from different directions at different times of the year, causing wet and dry seasons.

moraine   Piles of boulders, rock, pebbles and clay carried by a glacier or left behind after a glacier has melted.

oasis   A moist area in a desert where the water table reaches the surface.

oxygen   A gas in the Earth's atmosphere. Animals and plants need oxygen to break down their food and release energy for living and growing.

ozone layer   A layer of ozone gas (a form of oxygen) in the Earth's atmosphere which absorbs 90 percent of the harmful ultraviolet rays from the Sun.

planet   A large ball of rock, metal or gas that orbits a star. The Earth is a planet that orbits our Sun.

sediment   Rock debris, such as sand, mud or gravel, moved around by wind, water or ice.

sedimentary rock   A rock formed from the debris of other rocks, or from the remains of plants or animals.

star   A huge ball of gas in space, which gives out vast amounts of heat and light energy. The sun is a star.

sonar   A way of navigating underwater and detecting objects by sending out sound waves. The letters stand for SOund Navigation And Ranging.

stalactite   A long, thin piece of calcium carbonate hanging down from the roof of a cave. A stalactite looks like an icicle.

stalagmite   A column of calcium carbonate growing up from the floor of a cave.

subduction   The process by which one of the Earth's plates is forced beneath another as the two collide.

temperate climate   A climate that is neither very hot nor very cold, between the hot tropics and the cold poles.

tides   The regular rise and fall of the water in the oceans due to the pull of the Moon's and the Sun's gravity.

ultraviolet rays   Invisible rays given off by very hot objects, including the Sun. Ultraviolet rays can be harmful to your skin.

Universe   Everything that exists.

water table   The level in rocks below which the rock is saturated with (full of) water.

weathering   The gradual breaking down of rocks on the Earth's surface by the weather or by plants.

Index

Note: Page numbers in *italic* refer to information given only in boxes or in picture captions or labels.

EARTH FACTS

Circumference at the equator — about 40,200 km	**Hottest place** — 58°C in Libya	**Highest mountain on surface** — Chomolungma (Everest), Nepal, 8,848 m
Surface area — 510,000,000 km²	**Coldest place** — -89.2°C at Vostok Station, Antarctica	**Longest river** — River Nile, Egypt, over 6,400 km long
Mass — 6,588,000,000,000,000,000,000 tonnes	**Windiest place** — winds reaching 320 km per hour at George V Coast, Antarctica	**Largest desert** — Sahara Desert, Africa, 9,000,000 km²
Surface area covered by land — 149,000,000 km²	**Most snow on ground** — 1,146 cm in March 1911, at Tamarack, California	**Highest waterfall** — Angel Falls, Venezuela, 979 m
Surface area covered by oceans — 228,527,000 km²	**Driest place** — Atacama Desert, Chile – 0.008 cm a year	**Largest freshwater lake** — Lake Superior, North America, 83,243 km²
Largest ocean (Pacific) — 361,000,000 km²	**Largest hailstone** — 1 kg in Gopalganj district, Bangladesh	**Largest iceberg ever recorded** — 31,000 km² – larger than Belgium
Largest continent (Asia) — 44,387,000 km² in area	**Sunniest place** — Yuma, Arizona, with an average of 4,127 hours of bright sunlight each year	**Longest glacier** — Lambert Glacier in Antarctica, about 400 km long
Movement of the Earth's plates — 2–20 cm per year		
Highest annual average rainfall — 1,187.5 cm at Mawsynram, India		

PICTURE ACKNOWLEDGEMENTS

ARTWORK

Richard Bonson, 10 (below left), 14 (top left), 17 (top left and right), 25 (right); **Eugene Fleury** (maps), 20–21, 23, 37, 63; **Mike Foster** (Maltings Partnership), 14–15, 62 (top right), 64–65; **Gary Hincks,** 34–35, 38–39 (centre), 40–41 (centre), 42–43, 50–51, 52–53, 54–55; **Rob Jakeway,** 29, (below right); **Eric Robson,** 20–21, 32 (top left), 48–49; **Peter Sarson and Richard Chasemore,** 12 (below left), 13 (right), 16 (top left), 16 (centre right), 17 (centre), 18 (below right), 19 (top right), 29 (top right), 24 (top right), 25 (below left), 26 (below right), 27 (top right), 29 (top right), 30-31, 33, 36, 39 (centre right), 40 (below left), 41 (right), 42 (top right), 44–45, 47 (right inset), 49 (top right), 57 (below right), 58–59, 61 (top), 65 (centre right); **Roger Stewart,** 8–9, 10–11, 12–13 (centre), 16–17, 18–19 (centre), 22–23, 24–25, 26–27, 28–29, 32, 46–47, 56–57, 60–61, 62; **Colin Woolf,** 37, 54 (below left), 59 (centre right).

PHOTOGRAPHS

Endpapers: Zefa Pictures; 4 Stuart Westmorland/Tony Stone Images; 7 The Natural History Museum, London; 8 NASA; 9 Mike Agliolo/Science Photo Library; 11 NASA; 17 Arnulf Husmo/Tony Stone Images; 18 Arthur Pengelly/Dominion News; 19 Suzanne Aitzetmuller/Oxford Scientific Films; 21 Jane Burton/Bruce Coleman; 22 Adrian Warren/Ardea; 27 (left) The Natural History Museum, London; 27 (right) Bruce Davidson/Oxford Scientific Films; 28 Steven C. Kaufman/Bruce Coleman; 30 Susan Meiselas/Magnum Photos; 33 Zefa Pictures; 34 Geospace/Science Photo Library; 36 Pierre Jaunet/Aspect Picture Library; 38 NASA/Science Photo Library; 40 Steve McCurry/Magnum Photos; 44 NOAA/Science Photo Library; 46 Julia Bayne/Robert Harding Picture Library; 46–47 Paul Harris/Royal Geographical Society; 50–51 CNES, 1990 Distribution Spot Image/Science Photo Library; 51 David Parker/Science Photo Library; 52 Larry Ulrich/Tony Stone Images; 53 Jeffrey Brown/Frank Spooner Pictures; 54 Ben Osborne/Oxford Scientific Films; 56 Zefa Pictures; 58 Robert Gibbs/Impact Photos; 60 Doug Perrine/Planet Earth Pictures; 62 Tom van Sant/Geosphere Project, Santa Monica/Science Photo Library; 64 Will & Deni McIntyre/ Science Photo Library; 65 Peter Menzel/Science Photo Library